my Christian Faith

Response Book

CONCORDIA PUBLISHING HOUSE • SAINT LOUIS

Written by David Anderson, Jill Anthony, Thomas Couser, Daniel Czaplewski, Bruce Frederickson, Charles Groth, Jeanette Groth, Don Krogstad, James Metcalf, William Moorhead, Kevin Popp, Eileen Ritter, Greg Sawyer, Richard Schmidt, Erik Thomack, Sheila Thomack, Darrell Zimmerman

Edited by Rodney L. Rathmann and Kenneth C. Wagener

Photo credits: Norhill—8, 12, 18, 22, 24, 27, 31, 32, 34, 43, 56, 64, 65, 74, 77, 93, 94, 95, 107, 110, 112; Image Club Graphics, Inc.—47; Skjold Photographs—57, 90, 98; CPH—109.

Write to Library for the Blind, 1333 S. Kirkwood Road, St. Louis, MO 63122-7295 to obtain *My Christian Faith* (Response Book) in Braille or in large type for the visually impaired.

8   9   10   11   12   13   14   15   12   11   10   09   08   07   06   05

Contents

1

The Christian Faith

Introduction

Lost and Found

[Jesus said,] "Suppose a woman has ten silver coins and loses one. Does she not light a lamp, sweep the house and search carefully until she finds it? And when she finds it, she calls her friends and neighbors together and says, 'Rejoice with me; I have found my lost coin.' In the same way, I tell you, there is rejoicing in the presence of the angels of God over one sinner who repents." Luke 15:8–10

Share with your group a time when you were younger and became lost.

_____

_____

_____

How did you feel when you first realized you were lost?

_____

_____

_____

In what way are people who don't know Jesus "lost"?

_____

_____

_____

In the parable that Jesus told, the woman is like God. How does God feel about lost people and what has He done to find them?

_____

_____

_____

_____

The Shepherd and His Sheep

[Jesus said,] "I am the good shepherd; I know My sheep and My sheep know Me—just as the Father knows Me and I know the Father—and I lay down My life for the sheep" (John 10:14–15).

Use paper and markers to draw a poster picture of this Bible passage. Be sure to include in your illustration the Father, the Shepherd (Jesus) and yourself, one of His sheep.

God's People Make Choices

These people faced real life situations that called on them to make tough decisions. Choose one of the passages listed and answer the following questions for the situation the people faced.

Joseph	Genesis 39:5–10
Rahab	Joshua 2:1–7, Hebrews 11:31
Daniel	Daniel 6:6–10
Andrew, Peter, James, and John	Matthew 4:18–22
Paul and Silas	Acts 16:22–28, 29–34

1. What choice did the follower of God face?

_____

_____

_____

_____

Joseph and Rahab, Heroes of Faith by the Grace of God

2. How did his or her faith in God influence his or her decision?

_____

_____

_____

3. What did he or she decide to do?

_____

_____

_____

4. How did it turn out in the end?

_____

_____

_____

Time for Reflection

Complete the following information about yourself. Then respond to the questions about your Christian faith right now. You may want to refer to what you have written sometime in the future.

The Growing Family

- Interview your parent or parents using the questions on the Activity Sheet. Sign and date on the spaces provided after completing your interview. Keep this sheet with your Response Book to reflect upon in the future.

- Ask your parents to tell you their goals for your participation in this confirmation study program. Consider together, **How will we know one year from now that this confirmation program has been a success?** With your parents, establish one or two goals to share with the pastor by the next session.

- Ask your parents to tell you what their relationship with Jesus Christ means to them in their daily lives. Tell your parents what being a follower of Jesus means to you.

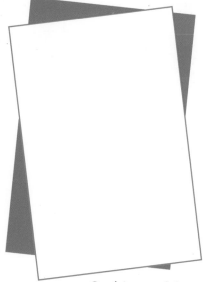

God Loves Me

With My Mentor

- Ask your mentor for a favorite Bible passage that helps him or her understand the heart of the Christian faith. What passage best explains the way of salvation and offers words to live by?

- Ask your mentor to share with you a recent major decision. Ask him or her to share how faith in Christ helped influence the decision and how he or she felt after the decision was made. Talk about how a strong and informed faith helps a Christian make tough decisions.

Name:_____ Age:_____

Church affiliation _____

Pastor: _____

Others in your class: _____

_____

_____

_____

_____

In what ways is your Christian faith important to you?

_____

_____

_____

_____

_____

_____

What plans do you have for your personal relationship with Jesus Christ in the future?

_____

_____

_____

_____

_____

Write a prayer, thanking God for the gift of faith that He has given you. Sign and date what you have written.

_____

_____

_____

_____

_____

_____

_____

_____

_____

_____

Name:_____ Date:_____

2

Priority One

The First Commandment

By Faith We Belong to God

Then Jesus told him, "Because you have seen Me, you have believed; blessed are those who have not seen and yet have believed." John 20:29

Jesus did many other miraculous signs in the presence of His disciples, which are not recorded in this book. But these are written that you may believe that Jesus is the Christ, the Son of God, and that by believing you may have life in His name. John 20:29–31

What Do We Believe?

It was Saturday. Jake and Antheis sat waiting for the rehearsal to begin. Tomorrow their spring community concert would be held in this church—St. John Lutheran—the biggest Lutheran church in the city. As they sat admiring the size and beauty of the new structure, Andy walked over and sat by them. Several minutes later, he joined in their conversation by asking the question, "What do Lutherans believe?" If you were Jake or Antheis, how would you answer Andy's question?

_____

_____

_____

You shall have no other
gods.

What does this mean? We
should fear, love, and trust
in God above all things.

Two Young Lives

Ama Wowana trusts in Jesus as her Savior, and though she is sometimes afraid, she feels she has to do what she knows to be right. Though the political majority in her country has succeeded in passing laws that persecute Christians, Ama refuses to hide what Jesus means to her. Ama knows that refusing to keep her faith a secret could disqualify her from many privileges including the field of study she would most like to pursue for a career. Ama and her Christian friends face their situation confidently.

Regularly, they meet together to praise and worship Jesus for living, dying, and living again for them. Together they find comfort, direction, and encouragement through their study of God's Word and in their conversations with one another about how God is working in their individual lives. Ironically, the group of Christians in their country is thriving under persecution.

Though the same age as Ama, most everything about Brian is different from Ama. Brian lives in New York, on the other side of the globe from Ama's home. Here everyone is free to worship as he or she pleases.

Brian's family members have been Christians for many generations. Though he was brought up in the church, these days Brian attends church infrequently. He usually goes to church with his family just to carry on a Christmas, Easter, and Thanksgiving tradition.

Brian always identifies himself as a Lutheran when asked about his religious affiliation, but he doesn't think much about the faith into which he was confirmed. Only when he fears the possibility of something dreadful happening does he pray. "Jesus is something for little kids to believe in," Brian once said to a friend.

For Reflection

1. Contrast the blessings God has given Ama with those He has given to Brian.

_____

_____

_____

_____

_____

2. The Christian church often thrives during times of persecution. Why do you think this is true?

_____

_____

_____

_____

_____

3. Which of these two young people reminds you most of the place God occupies in your life right now? Explain.

_____

_____

_____

_____

Here I Stand!

God Helps Us to Put Him First

On an afternoon in April 1521, Martin Luther, respected pastor and teacher, stood in the middle of the great castle hall at Worms, Germany. In his many writings, Luther had criticized the leaders of the church for their mistaken views. He insisted that God's Word was reliable: we are saved by God's grace alone, because of Christ's death and resurrection. Some people, however, taught that true faith was not enough: people must also work for their salvation, to make certain that God's forgiveness is complete.

The emperor demanded once more. "Do you wish to recall and retract your books and all the errors of your teachings?"

Luther realized the serious nature of his situation. His next words were critical. In the past, men and women had been killed for their refusal to follow the authority of the church.

"Since you ask for a simple answer, I will give it: Unless I am convinced by the testimony of the Scriptures … I am bound by the Scriptures I have quoted and my conscience is captive to the Word of God. I

The Growing Family

• With your family reflect upon the commandment, "You shall have no other gods." Share what Jesus' life, death, and resurrection mean for you. Talk about the ways you, either individually or as a family, can show your desire to "fear, love, and trust in God above all things."

- Ask members of your family to select objects from your immediate surroundings to use as visual aids to share what God and His goodness mean to them. For example, a light could remind someone that Jesus is the Light of the world, food items may help someone think about how God continues to provide for us, a doorway or hallway could be reminiscent of Jesus, the only way to eternal life. After everyone has had an opportunity to share, conclude your devotional time with a prayer. Ask God to help you always to fear, love, and trust, in Him above all things.

With My Mentor

- Interview your mentor about ways he or she shows God to be "priority 1" in his or her daily life—at home and on the job.

- Contact your mentor by phone to encourage him or her in the desire to live the Christian faith. Pray with him or her over the phone, thanking God for His blessings and asking for His strength and power to help both of you to fear, love, and trust in Him above all things.

cannot and will not retract anything, since it is neither safe nor right to go against conscience."

God had made Luther's faith strong enough for him to risk everything for the sake of the Gospel. Luther knew that regardless of what might happen to him, he was a child of God by faith in Jesus the Savior who had lived, died, and rose again to earn forgiveness, new life, and an eternal home in heaven for him.

The following principles may be helpful as you prepare yourself to take a stand for your Savior.

- Read and study God's Word regularly and often.
- Choose friends who share your desire to live their life for the one true God.
- Avoid those influences that might tempt you to abandon your faith in Jesus.
- Talk to God often in prayer.
- Acknowledge that Christian values often run counter to those popular in society.
- Faithfully receive God's power through the Sacrament of the Altar.
- Memorize, "I can do everything through Him who gives me strength." (Philippians 4:13)

On the following lines, reflect on the good things God has brought to your life. Comment about the type of Christian you desire to be. Ask God to make you strong in living and speaking about the faith you profess. Sign and date your reflection.

Name:_____ Date:_____

3

A Name and Time for God

The Second Commandment
The Third Commandment

In Spirit and in Truth

Jesus declared, "Believe me, woman, a time is coming when you will worship the Father neither on this mountain nor in Jerusalem. You Samaritans worship what you do not know; we worship what we know, for salvation is from the Jews. Yet a time is coming and has now come when the true worshipers will worship the Father in spirit and truth, for they are the kind of worshipers the Father seeks. God is spirit, and His worshipers must worship in spirit and in truth." John 4:21–24

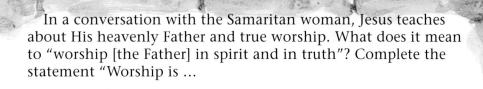

In a conversation with the Samaritan woman, Jesus teaches about His heavenly Father and true worship. What does it mean to "worship [the Father] in spirit and in truth"? Complete the statement "Worship is ...

_____

_____

_____

_____

A Name for God

What is God's name? The Bible presents a rich variety of names and titles to identify the true, living and eternal God. Each of the passages below offers a "story picture" of God.

Read the story and write down as many "names" for God as possible called to mind by the following events.

- God, Abraham, and Isaac: Genesis 22:1–18

_____

- God and Jacob: Genesis 28:10–22

_____

- God and Moses: Exodus 3:1–15

_____

- God and Samuel: 1 Samuel 3:1–21

_____

- God and Elijah: 1 Kings 19:9–18

_____

For Reflection

What words best describe God's presence in your life? In what ways does God's power and love strengthen you for daily living? Sign and date what you have written.

_____

_____

_____

_____

_____

_____

Name:_____ Date:_____

The Second Commandment

You shall not misuse the name of the Lord your God.

What does this mean? We should fear and love God so that we do not curse, swear, use satanic arts, lie, or deceive by His name, but call upon it in every trouble, pray, praise, and give thanks.

The Third Commandment

Remember the Sabbath day by keeping it holy.

What does this mean? We should fear and love God so that we do not despise preaching and His Word, but hold it sacred and gladly hear and learn it.

Design Your Day

My Activities	Time Spent	Service to God

Service with a Smile

The Garaway family walked to the corner table with a look of contentment and anticipation. Pastor Bill, his wife Martha, and two daughters Sarah and Elizabeth, decided to celebrate Sarah's baptismal birthday at one of Middleton's nicer restaurants. Both girls were excited to be able to order their favorite menu item—fish and chips.

As Janel, their waitress, wrote down the last of the family's menu selections and turned back to the kitchen with the order, Pastor Garaway asked, "How is our dinner tonight like Sunday morning worship?"

"Oh, Dad!," the two sisters exclaimed together, in mock exasperation.

"You never miss an opportunity, do you?" his wife gently teased.

"Well, this one's too good to pass up," the pastor responded. "There's something here I want all of us to remember about worship. So, girls, what do you think? How is our time in this restaurant this evening going to be like Sunday morning worship?"

Sarah and Elizabeth looked at each other, then back at their father. "Couldn't you please give us a hint?" asked Elizabeth.

"Okay," responded Pastor Garaway. "It has something to do with what our waitress will soon be doing at this table."

The Growing Family

- Write each family member's name on a note card and place the cards on the table. Look at one card at a time and share how you honor that person's name and identity. Write the name of Jesus on a note card. Ask each member of your family to share how he/she shows honor and respect for Christ.

- Invite the members of your family to write on a note card the most meaningful part of last Sunday's worship service. Allow each person to share and to react to other responses.

With My Mentor

- Write two important truths from the Second and Third Commandments. Call your mentor and share your thoughts on honoring God in worship, and in your speech and actions.

- Read and discuss John 4:21–24 with your mentor. Talk about the great God and Savior and the privilege we have of worshiping Him in spirit and in truth.

"I think I know," said Sarah. "She's going to bring us our meals."

"That's right," said her father. "Now, how is that like Sunday morning?"

"Well," Mrs. Garaway said, "God feeds us with His Word. And Christ gives His body and blood for us to eat and drink together with the bread and wine."

"Exactly!" Pastor Garaway smiled. "In fact, at worship God first serves us. He gives to us through His Word—when we hear the Scripture lessons read, when we sing hymns, when we hear the sermon preached. God is serving us. And Jesus serves us in a very special way when we take the bread and wine, His body and blood, in the Lord's Supper. That's why we call worship a 'service.' In the service God is serving us."

Elizabeth turned to Sarah. "I think I'm going to be hearing more about this in confirmation class," she said.

"Yes, you will," replied Pastor Garaway. "We'll learn more about worship and God's gifts to us in Word and Sacrament."

Just then the waitress arrived with a basket of hot garlic bread and cheese bits. "Okay," she said cheerily. "Here we go. Now, who wants the appetizers?" Both Sarah and Elizabeth raised their hands high.

"Happy Baptism Birthday, Sarah," said her mother, "and God bless and serve you always!"

For Reflection

1. How does God serve us in the worship service?

_____

_____

_____

_____

2. How are we to receive such service from God?

_____

_____

_____

_____

3. How does this view of the worship service agree with Luther's explanations of the Second and Third Commandments?

_____

_____

_____

_____

4

God's Representatives

The Fourth Commandment

Relationships in the Lord

Submit to one another out of reverence for Christ. Children, obey your parents in the Lord, for this is right. "Honor your father and mother"—which is the first commandment with a promise—"that it may go well with you and that you may enjoy long life on the earth." Fathers, do not exasperate your children; instead, bring them up in the training and instruction of the Lord. Ephesians 5:21; 6:1–4

What does St. Paul mean by "obey your parents in the Lord"?

_____

_____

_____

_____

Who's in Charge?

Complete this ideagram following the instructions your teacher will give you.

The Fourth Commandment

Honor your father and your mother.

What does this mean? We should fear and love God so that we do not despise or anger our parents and other authorities, but honor them, serve and obey them, love and cherish them.

Parents Are Children Too

As Michelle walked into the kitchen, her mother was on the phone. Evalyn wasn't talking, however; she was listening. Michelle quietly placed her book bag on the kitchen table. Mother turned toward her junior high daughter and whispered, "Hi, honey."

Michelle was hungry. It had been a long, hot September day at Nelson Middle School. She opened the refrigerator door and silently pondered the items on the shelves. Waves of cold air spilled over her arms and face. "This sure feels good," she thought to herself, "but Dad would say our electric bill is high enough as it is." She quickly decided on a small jar of applesauce, and getting a spoon from the drawer, sat down at the kitchen table. She pushed her book bag to one side and waited for her mother to get off the phone. Michelle had promised to call her girlfriend Karen right after school. She wanted to call before starting her homework.

When her mother hung up the phone, she turned to Michelle. "How was your day today?"

"Nothing spectacular." Just then she saw her mother wipe a small tear from the corner of her eye. "Is something wrong, Mom?"

"Well, yes there is," her mother replied with a sigh. "Grandma hasn't been doing too well on her own in the apartment the past few weeks. I've suggested that she move into a care home, but I don't feel very good about that either. I don't know exactly what to do, and, of course, Grandma thinks she's just fine where she is. I worry about her. And I worry about the decision I'm trying to help her make. She's my mother, but now I find that I need to take care of her! It's a tall order to be parent to your own parent."

Michelle thought for a moment. "What do you think will finally happen with Grandma?" Michelle asked.

"I suppose Grandma will eventually move into the care home. I just hope that by then we're both more comfortable with the idea. I really do love her. She has taken care of me all these years, and now she's counting on me to take care of her.

Michelle's mother paused. "Maybe someday you'll be faced with the same problem," she said anxiously.

Michelle smiled. "Then I hope I'm ready for the responsibility, too!"

For Reflection

Complete the following. Include your signature and today's date at the end of the section.

1. If I were Michelle, my concerns would be ...

_____

_____

2. If I were Evalyn, my concerns would be ...

_____

_____

3. As a Christian, I show honor to my parent(s) by ...

_____

_____

4. One thing I admire about the parent(s) God has given me is:

_____

_____

Place a photo of your family here.

My Family

Signed:_____ Date:_____

The Growing Family

- Together with your family, browse through the photographs and mementos in your family albums. Share interesting stories, facts and insights from the past. Encourage each other to appreciate your family's unique history and blessings from God. Pray together thanking God for your family.

- Watch your favorite television shows and evaluate parent-child relationships. Are there positive role models? Negative models? How does each show demonstrate—or fail to demonstrate—God's will as revealed in the Fourth Commandment?

With My Mentor

- Discuss with your mentor a recent local or national event involving a prominent authority figure. Was it a positive witness? a negative witness? From the perspective of the Fourth Commandment, what is an appropriate Christian response to this authority figure?

- Locate and clip recent newspaper and magazine articles that relate to parent-child relationships or other authority situations. With your mentor, discuss these stories in light of the Fourth Commandment.

5

Life Matters

The Fifth Commandment

Murder One

The God who made the world and everything in it is the Lord of heaven and earth and does not live in temples built by hands. And He is not served by human hands, as if He needed anything, because He Himself gives all men life and breath and everything else. From one man He made every nation of men, that they should inhabit the whole earth; and He determined the times set for them and the exact places where they should live. God did this so that men would seek Him and perhaps reach out for Him and find Him, though He is not far from each one of us. Acts 17:24–27

Murder! The word itself sounds harsh. We describe murder in graphic language: vicious, grisly, brutal.

Murder is horrible because a wrongful death cannot be undone. No punishment, insurance settlement, or other compensation can ever restore a life that has been taken. It is no surprise that God should forbid such a crime. God is the Creator. The psalmist writes, "Know that the LORD is God. *It is He who made us,* and we are His." (Psalm 100:3, emphasis added)

God alone gives life. The Creator of the universe also reserves the right to take life.

The first murder was committed by the oldest child of Adam and Eve. Read Genesis 4:1–16.

1. What might Cain have felt toward his brother?

_____

_____

_____

_____

2. What has been the most famous murder in your lifetime? Why was it so famous?

_____

_____

_____

_____

3. Make a list of words to describe your feelings about murder.

_____

_____

_____

_____

Alive and Well

The story of Cain and Abel did not have to end in murder. Because of pride, jealousy, and anger, Cain killed his brother.

Sin destroys relationships. Because of sin we are separated from God and from one another. We are, by nature, enemies of God and alienated from all other human beings.

Jesus Christ, however, forgives, heals, and restores relationships. In His death and resurrection we have been forgiven and brought together in love and peace. We accept one another, because our Lord has first accepted us.

Think again of the story of Cain and Abel. How might the story have been different with the forgiveness and love of Christ present …

The Fifth Commandment

You shall not murder.

What does this mean? We should fear and love God so that we do not hurt or harm our neighbor in his body, but help and support him in every physical need.

21

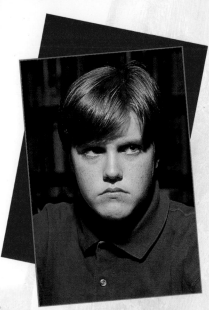

The Growing Family

• Have a family devotional time to discuss anger and how each person manages and resolves anger. On a sheet of paper, folded in half (lengthwise) to make two columns, have family members write—on the left side—specific events or conflicts from the past week that made them angry. In the right column, have family members write their responses to the situations.

As you read Ephesians 4:26, discuss how anger can be dealt with in a God-pleasing way. Join in a prayer, asking God's forgiveness for past sins, and His strength to live as forgiven, forgiving people.

As a family discuss your feelings about: life support systems; living wills; organ donation. If you wish, review some possible living wills and make one. Consider filling out an organ donor card.

The Anger Ladder

I become angry when ...

_____

_____

_____

When angry, I ...

_____

_____

_____

When someone is angry with me, I ...

_____

_____

_____

I deal with my anger by ...

_____

_____

_____

"You have heard that it was said to the people long ago, 'Do not murder, and anyone who murders will be subject to judgment.' But I tell you that anyone who is angry with his brother will be subject to judgment. Again, anyone who says to his brother, 'Raca,' is answerable to the Sanhedrin. But anyone who says, 'You fool!' will be in danger of the fire of hell." (Matthew 5:21–22)

"In your anger do not sin": Do not let the sun go down while you are still angry, and do not give the devil a foothold. (Ephesians 4:26–27)

Precious in His Sight

Build Us Up

Years ago, the world watched as three gray whales, trapped by ice near Point Barrow, Alaska, struggled for life. Battered and bleeding, the whales gasped for breath at every hole in the ice. But the open sea was five miles away. The only hope for survival was to lead the three whales to freedom—one hole at a time.

Rescuers began cutting a string of breathing holes twenty yards apart in the six-inch ice cover. For eight days, they coaxed the whales from one hole to the next, mile after mile. Along the way, one of the three vanished. For a time, the other two seemed lost.

But finally, with the help of a Russian icebreaker, the whales—named by now Putu and Siku—swam to freedom.

(adapted from "Illustrations for Preaching and Teaching" from *Leadership Journal* edited by Craig Larson, Baker Books, Div., of Baker Book House Co., © 1993.)

"Help and support." God's Spirit empowers Jesus' faithful disciples to share His love through our words and actions to all people. In His strength, we build each other up for faithful service to God and the world.

Therefore encourage one another and build each other up, just as in fact you are doing. (1 Thessalonians 5:11)

Looks Like	Sounds Like

Encouragement is best practiced first among those closest to us. Write a paragraph that tells how, by the Spirit's power, you can show God's love in the way you treat your siblings and/or close friends. Sign and date what you have written.

_____

_____

_____

_____

_____

_____

_____

Signed:_____ Date:_____

- Allow time for every member of the family to share with every other member an encouraging word about one thing he or she especially appreciates about him or her. Then join together in prayer, thanking God for your family, and asking His blessing as you grow together in Christian love and faith in Him.

With My Mentor

- Ask your mentor to share his or her appreciation for life as a gift from God. Where possible, reflect upon past examples of God's goodness and protection in times of hardship or danger. Share your own understanding of God's love in Christ, and the ways He has guided your life.

- Share with your mentor your life's goals and plans. Invite him or her to pray with you for God's guidance, protection, and blessings as you plan—and live—your life for Him.

6

Faithful for Life

The Sixth Commandment

Male and Female—In God's Image

[Jesus replied,] "But at the beginning of creation God 'made them male and female.' 'For this reason a man will leave his father and mother and be united to his wife, and the two will become one flesh.' So they are no longer two, but one. Therefore what God has joined together, let man not separate." Mark 10:6–9

"Very Good"

Can you imagine what life would be like with only females? or only males? Not good! But for a brief time, on the sixth day of creation, God's work was unfinished. The first man, Adam, was alone in the Garden of Eden. In spite of God's abundant blessing, living in a perfect paradise, the situation was not good. Even God acknowledged, "It is not good for the man to be alone" (Genesis 2:18).

So God caused Adam to fall into a deep sleep and removed part of his side. The Lord created another human being—the first woman. When the man awoke, God brought His new creation to Adam.

"This is now bone of my bones and flesh of my flesh; she shall be called 'woman' for she was taken out of man" (Genesis 2:23).

God spoke His blessing as He revealed His will for male and female. "For this reason a man will leave his father and mother and be united to his wife, and they will become one flesh" (Genesis 2:24).

God's plan is for man and woman to leave their parents and establish a new home and a new family. They are united as husband and wife, just like Adam and Eve. Marriage is God's way to bless His creation, to provide for happiness and fulfillment, and to bring forth children for generation after generation.

It's a very good gift from God.

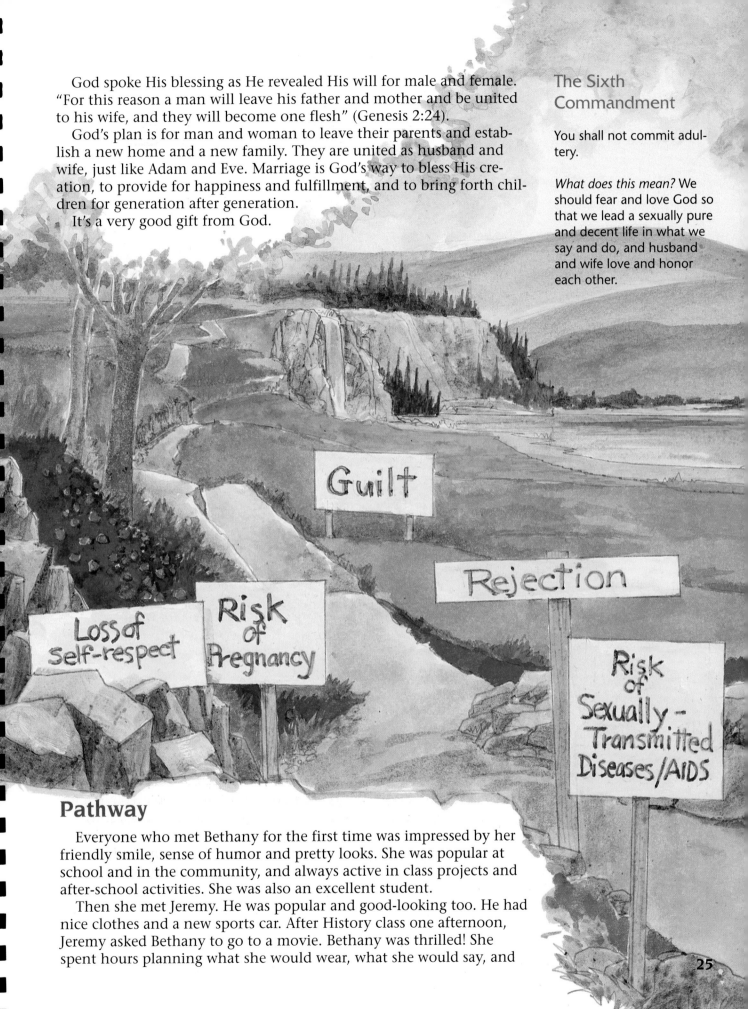

Guilt

Rejection

Loss of Self-respect

Risk of Pregnancy

Risk of Sexually-Transmitted Diseases/AIDS

Pathway

Everyone who met Bethany for the first time was impressed by her friendly smile, sense of humor and pretty looks. She was popular at school and in the community, and always active in class projects and after-school activities. She was also an excellent student.

Then she met Jeremy. He was popular and good-looking too. He had nice clothes and a new sports car. After History class one afternoon, Jeremy asked Bethany to go to a movie. Bethany was thrilled! She spent hours planning what she would wear, what she would say, and how she would act on the date. It was an honor to be seen with Jeremy. He was a high school junior; she was in ninth grade. Yet Bethany knew she was on the way to the top!

The evening started fine. Jeremy talked freely, though mostly about himself. Still, he complimented Bethany several times and seemed genuinely interested in her. After the movie, they drove around for a while. Jeremy pulled into a quiet park and turned off the ignition.* Bethany was nervous but did not want to appear "immature" on their special date. For the first time in her life, Bethany had sexual intercourse. So, too, did Jeremy.

Jeremy drove home in complete silence. Bethany also said nothing. He stopped in front of her house and waited for Bethany to get out. They sat together for a few moments. Bethany had given Jeremy something she valued greatly, the most intimate part of herself. She wondered, "Do I mean anything to him?" Opening the door, Bethany left the car and headed toward the front steps of her home. She stopped, and turned toward Jeremy.

"Does this mean we're going together?" she asked softly.

"No. I'll see you around," Jeremy replied. He drove away.

- What were the positive points as Bethany and Jeremy began their relationship?

_____

_____

- What was different after they had sex? Why was their relationship different?

_____

_____

- On the "pathway" above, chart out the obstacles and problems that Bethany faces in the future.
- Chart out the obstacles and problems that Jeremy faces in the future.

Love Lines

Love	**Lust**

Heart to Heart

A father handed the car keys to his son, and wished the boy a pleasant, safe evening.

"By the way, do you think you will marry this girl you are dating tonight?" he inquired.

"Oh, Dad," replied the son, "what kind of question is that?"

"I'm serious. Do you think you will marry her?"

"Of course not. We're just going to have fun!"

"But you think you will get married to someone some day."

"Yeah, probably. I guess so."

"Then is it reasonable to think that your future wife might also be going out on a date tonight."

"Yeah. I suppose she might be going out tonight."

"How do you want the boy she is dating to treat her?"

"He better keep his hands off her."

The father remained quiet.

"Don't worry, Dad," responded the son. "I understand."

What was the father's point?

_____

_____

_____

What does God desire for your sexuality today and always? Write your response below. Sign and date your work.

_____

_____

_____

_____

_____

_____

Signed:_____ Date:_____

The Growing Family

- Ask your parents or another couple about the circumstances of their first meeting or date. If possible, find "old" photographs from the early years of their engagement or marriage. Invite both individuals to share their experiences—the blessings and challenges—of dating and life together as husband and wife.

- Develop a "Viewer Guide" for television programs. If you wish, use the traditional "G," "PG," "PG-13," and "R" classification. For each category, list positive or negative values and issues. Write down the names of 15–20 regular shows and rank each program according to your viewer guide. If possible, involve the whole family for a week; then discuss your rankings and reactions.

With My Mentor

- Discuss what is appropriate behavior for two Christians on a date and how to avoid awkward circumstances and sexual temptations on dates.

- Together with your mentor pray for the person you will one day marry, asking God to bless him or her right now with experiences through which he or she will grow closer to God and prepare him or her to be a faithful and godly spouse.

7

Possessions: Yours and Mine

The Seventh Commandment

True Treasure

[Jesus said,] "Do not be afraid, little flock, for your Father has been pleased to give you the kingdom. Sell your possessions and give to the poor. Provide purses for yourselves that will not wear out, a treasure in heaven that will not be exhausted, where no thief comes near and no moth destroys. For where your treasure is, there your heart will be also." Luke 12:32–34

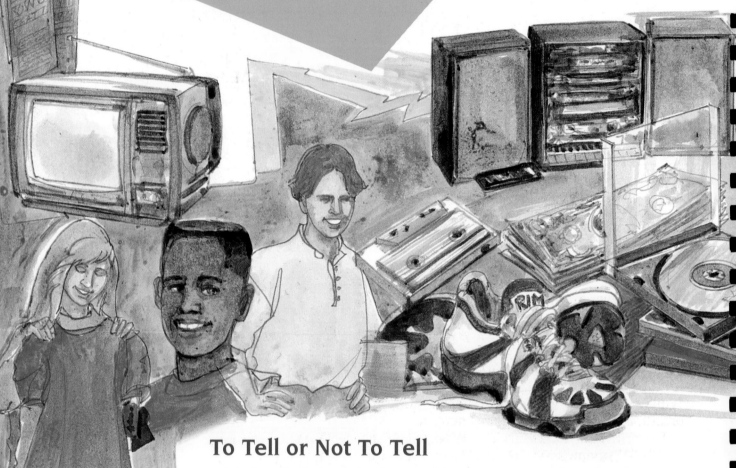

To Tell or Not To Tell

Mark walked slowly back toward homeroom. He often slipped away by himself after lunch, because his next class was Algebra. He also wanted to avoid Bruce. Lately, Bruce had been relentless—constantly teasing and bullying Mark. Bruce had even threatened Mark on occasion. Whenever possible, Mark did his best to stay away from Bruce.

As he opened the door to the room, Mark froze. There was Bruce—standing behind Mrs. William's desk, holding her wallet! With lightning speed, Bruce stuffed the bills into his pockets, snapped shut the wallet, and tossed it into the purse. He quickly opened the desk drawer and jammed the purse inside.

Mark started out the door.

"Mark!" Bruce growled.

Mark stopped. All at once Bruce had Mark pinned to the wall.

"If you ever say anything ..."

Mark remained motionless. When Bruce walked away, Mark took a deep breath. He understood, alright. Bruce was not kidding, and certainly would follow through on his threat.

Mark was perplexed! He turned away and walked quietly to the restroom. What should he do? Think! Let it go, he thought. Mrs. Williams probably would not miss the money. He took another deep breath, and headed again for homeroom.

The principal stood with Mrs. Williams outside the homeroom door!

"Mark!" boomed Mr. Smith's voice. "I'd like to talk with you a minute."

Mark walked slowly toward Mr. Smith.

"It seems that Mrs. Williams has lost some money," the principal said. "You were seen with her purse. Do you know anything about this?"

The Seventh Commandment

You shall not steal.

What does this mean? We should fear and love God so that we do not take our neighbor's money or possessions, or get them in any dishonest way, but help him to improve and protect his possessions and income.

The Growing Family

• Share God's love with your parents by doing something unexpected for them without being asked to help them improve their property and possessions. Possibilities may include washing the car(s), cleaning the garage, or tidying up the kitchen.

• Ask your parents to tell you about their prized possessions when they were your age. Tell them which of your possessions you value most. Together thank God for the many blessings He continues to provide.

1. What are Mark's options?

_____

_____

2. What would you do in Mark's situation?

_____

_____

3. How, as Mark's friend, might you support him through this ordeal?

_____

Why Steal?

Why steal? A thief may offer many reasons—excuses—for stealing. Write some likely responses to the question, "Why steal?"

_____

_____

_____

_____

What types of items are commonly stolen? Why?

_____

_____

_____

_____

Stealing is wrong. The Seventh Commandment forbids taking what does not rightly and legally belong to us.

Stealing, of course, is not simply burglary or shoplifting. "You shall not steal" means that God forbids "every kind of robbery, theft, and dishonest way of getting things."

Every person, at one time or another, is guilty of stealing—literally! We have taken what belongs to others, or have not helped to improve and protect our neighbor's possession. We have sinned against God and against one another. We deserve punishment for our sins.

Thank God!, however, that Jesus Christ is our Savior and friend. By His death and resurrection, He has removed the "guilty" verdict against us and taken upon Himself our punishment. His sacrifice is our hope for forgiveness and eternal salvation. In Christ, we are God's people. By the Holy Spirit we are empowered to live as people of integrity.

When Satan tempts us to take what does not belong to us we *can* resist with God's help. God has promised to be with us. Further, as His children we can work together, support, and encourage each other.

When you're tempted (before you're tempted!) consider the following:

Pray for God's forgiveness for times you have sinned.

Pray daily for the Spirit's guidance in your life. Ask for God's strength to resist temptation.

Seek advice and encouragement from a parent, youth sponsor, youth minister, director of Christian education, teacher, or pastor.

Commit yourself to regular Bible reading. The Lord speaks to you through His Word.

Surround yourself with friends committed to helping you grow in your faith.

Consider the joy we have as Christians in knowing that in Jesus there is forgiveness and hope. He calls us by the Gospel. In other words, we hear the *good news* of God's grace shown to us through Jesus when we read His Holy Word and hear it preached to us at worship. By the power of the Holy Spirit poured out on you at your Baptism, you have the power to live a new life in Christ. What does He call you to do with your faith? How can you as a teenager make a difference in your home, in your church, in your community? How can you improve your neighbor's life and property?

As an individual, as a class, as a group, consider these questions carefully. Make a plan. Write it out below and carry it out. In doing so we show the love of God to others who may not know Him!

My commitment to living my faith. With the help of the Holy Spirit I will …

_____

_____

_____

_____

_____

_____

_____

Signed:_____ Date:_____

With My Mentor

- Discuss with your mentor opportunities to be a young man or woman of integrity in the way we regard the property and possessions of others. Pray together asking God's forgiveness in Christ Jesus for past offenses and asking for the Spirit's power to do God's will as expressed in the Seventh Commandment.

- Together with your mentor, look for examples in the news that lend themselves to a discussion of the Seventh Commandment. Talk about positive applications of the Seventh Commandment in your everyday life.

31

8

A Good Reputation

The Eighth Commandment

Speaking the Truth in Love

Therefore each of you must put off falsehood and speak truthfully to his neighbor, for we are all members of one body. ... Do not let any unwholesome talk come out of your mouths, but only what is helpful for building others up according to their needs, that it may benefit those who listen. Ephesians 4:25, 29

False Witness

Heather was angry. She snapped at her brother, "Sticks and stones may break my bones, but words will never hurt me."

Yet inside she *was* hurt. Her brother's words had caused deep pain, especially since Heather's best friend Tammy heard everything.

"How could he say that I did not want to see her," she thought. "I stayed at home because I had to get my homework done!"

Heather was broken-hearted. Her brother had completely misrepresented why she had stayed away from all her friends the night before. He made it appear that Heather was *deliberately* avoiding Tammy and her other friends.

The next day, Tammy did see Heather at the lockers. She said, "Don't worry, I know that you're my friend. I have a lot of fun when I'm with you, and I know that you feel the same way about spending time with me. I'm sure glad we moved into your neighborhood when we came to town."

What might Heather's brother have said to her friends to give "false testimony" about his sister?

_____

_____

How did Tammy's remarks about their friendship "build up" Heather?

_____

_____

What is Jesus' truth for me? Write your own confession of sin against the Eighth Commandment and Jesus' promise to strengthen you. Sign and date your response.

_____

_____

_____

_____

_____

_____

_____

_____

Signed:_____ Date:_____

Absalom's Apple

You work for a company that operates a fruit stand in the neighborhood. Lately, sales and profits are good. One day you also decide to open a fruit stand in the neighborhood, but you do not want competition. Your solution? To undermine your current employer. You plan to make the fruit look beat up and bruised, so that people will stop coming to the fruit stand. Soon, you expect, your employer will go out of business. With competition out of the picture, you could open your own stand and start a profitable business.

The Bible presents a remarkable story of a son who plotted to destroy his father. Absalom, son of King David, sought to take the kingdom away from his father by capturing the hearts of the people. To win their affection, however, he had to give "false testimony" about himself and his father.

Read 2 Samuel 15:1–6.

1. In what ways does Absalom "lie?"

_____

_____

You shall not give false testimony against your neighbor.

What does this mean? We should fear and love God so that we do not tell lies about our neighbor, betray him, slander him, or hurt his reputation, but defend him, speak well of him, and explain everything in the kindest way.

The Growing Family

• Together with your family, explore the meaning of Jesus' saying on "specks" and "planks" (Luke 6:41–42). Discuss the ways we perceive and judge people based upon our values and attitudes.

• Ask family members to write down something of great value about their reputation. Allow time for sharing. Why is a good reputation important? Discuss ways that your family may defend, speak well of, and honor one another in word and deed.

• Make "Praise Tokens," the size of a quarter or half-dollar, from construction paper. Encourage family members to hand out the tokens as tangible expressions of gratitude and recognition for kindness during the week.

2. What do his words suggest about his father, King David?

_____

_____

3. How does the story of Absalom compare with the previous story?

_____

_____

Building Up Character

Janelle lives in an apartment building with her cat Missy. Missy recently gave birth to five lovely kittens. Janelle's neighbor heard about the kittens and asked if her young brother, Kevin, could come to see the kittens from time to time. Janelle agreed.

During Kevin's first visit, his older sister constantly reminds him, "Don't be rough with the kittens." She often comments, "Kevin, you're holding the kittens too tightly," or "I'm not going to bring you over anymore if you don't treat the kittens better."

Each time Kevin is criticized, he lowers his head, directs his eyes to the floor, and becomes quiet. His self-esteem diminishes. As Janelle watches Kevin, she notices that the kittens are safe and secure. Kevin is simply happy and wants to play with the furry animals. He is not rough or harsh. As Kevin's older sister stands by, Janelle affirms the young boy. "Kevin, look at how softly you treat the kittens. They must really like it when you pet them!"

As Janelle speaks, Kevin throws back his shoulders, breaks into a broad smile, and looks pleased.

What differences do you see between Janelle and Kevin's sister?

_____

_____

Why was Janelle able to build Kevin's self-confidence?

_____

_____

How did Kevin's sister miss the opportunity to "build up" Kevin?

_____

_____

With My Mentor

- With your mentor, share positive ways to defend and enhance another person's reputation.

- Ask your mentor to share with you a time from his or her experience when God's power enabled him or her to think or react to a situation "in the kindest way."

- Ask your mentor to share positive ways to defend and enhance another person's reputation.

9

God Provides

The Ninth Commandment
The Tenth Commandment

All Your Needs

I am not saying this because I am in need, for I have learned to be content whatever the circumstances. I know what it is to be in need, and I know what it is to have plenty. I have learned the secret of being content in any and every situation, whether well fed or hungry, whether living in plenty or in want. I can do everything through Him who gives me strength. ... And my God will meet all your needs according to His glorious riches in Christ Jesus. To our God and Father be glory for ever and ever. Amen. Philippians 4:11–13, 19–20

Wants and Wishes

Everyone dreams of the day. A shiny, new van pulls into the driveway, well-dressed men and women emerge, holding balloons and a large poster. A camera crew walks up the sidewalk. The doorbell rings. "Everything you want," they shout together, "all your wishes come true."

35

What would you wish for? Write your top five wishes below.

1.

2.

3.

4.

5.

It is, of course, not wrong to wish for something. Yet wishing for something we should not have or wishing for something inappropriately at the expense of someone else is sinful. It's called "coveting." The Bible includes many stories of people who coveted. They wanted, and in many cases attempted to get, what was not rightly their own.

Think of famous people from Bible times. As you watch the pantomimes, think about the following questions.

Who covets? What does he or she covet? How did he or she act upon their desires? What's the result?

What We Covet

Covetousness revolves around three distinct objects: the desire for power, for people, or for possessions. Read the following examples and match each with the appropriate category.

_____ 1. Janice cheated on her arithmetic test; she received the highest grade in her class.

_____ 2. Kim was running for class officer; she stole money from her mother's purse to buy ice cream sundaes for popular students.

_____ 3. Jack's parents couldn't afford expensive basketball shoes for him; he stole a pair from the gym where he works after school.

_____ 4. Tom told lies about Jeff to Lisa in hopes that she would like him better.

_____ 5. Bill spent part of his church offering for candy on the way to school.

_____ 6. Sarah smoked marijuana to get the attention of the boy next door.

People often covet because they confuse WANTS with NEEDS. Write a definition for each word:

WANTS

_____

_____

_____

NEEDS

_____

_____

_____

_____

The Ninth Commandment

You shall not covet your neighbor's house.

What does this mean? We should fear and love God so that we do not scheme to get our neighbor's inheritance or house, or get it in a way which only appears right, but help and be of service to him in keeping it.

The Tenth Commandment

You shall not covet your neighbor's wife, or his manservant or maidservant, his ox or donkey, or anything that belongs to your neighbor.

What does this mean? We should fear and love God so that we do not entice or force away our neighbor's wife, workers, or animals, or turn them against him, but urge them to stay and do their duty.

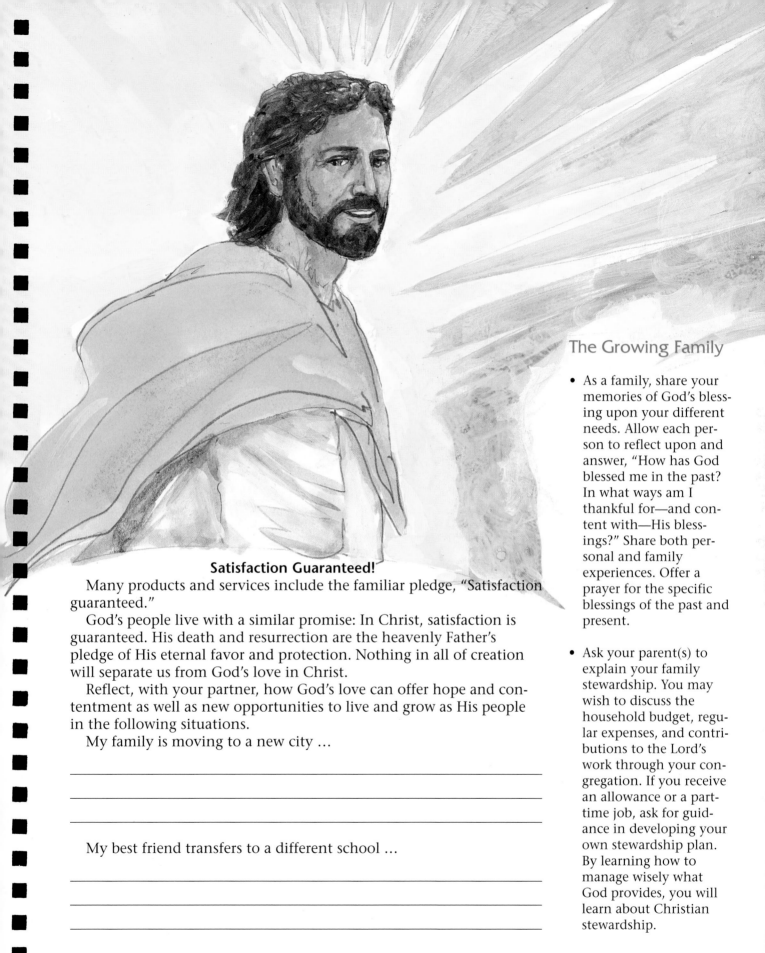

Satisfaction Guaranteed!

Many products and services include the familiar pledge, "Satisfaction guaranteed."

God's people live with a similar promise: In Christ, satisfaction is guaranteed. His death and resurrection are the heavenly Father's pledge of His eternal favor and protection. Nothing in all of creation will separate us from God's love in Christ.

Reflect, with your partner, how God's love can offer hope and contentment as well as new opportunities to live and grow as His people in the following situations.

My family is moving to a new city ...

_____

_____

_____

My best friend transfers to a different school ...

_____

_____

_____

The Growing Family

- As a family, share your memories of God's blessing upon your different needs. Allow each person to reflect upon and answer, "How has God blessed me in the past? In what ways am I thankful for—and content with—His blessings?" Share both personal and family experiences. Offer a prayer for the specific blessings of the past and present.

- Ask your parent(s) to explain your family stewardship. You may wish to discuss the household budget, regular expenses, and contributions to the Lord's work through your congregation. If you receive an allowance or a part-time job, ask for guidance in developing your own stewardship plan. By learning how to manage wisely what God provides, you will learn about Christian stewardship.

With My Mentor

- With your mentor explore together the different ways that you may be a "good steward" of God's gifts and still "make the most" of time with your friends and family.

- Ask your mentor whether he or she is content. Talk with him or her about the contentment God in Christ has brought to his or her life.

My team loses every game of the season …

_____
_____
_____
_____
_____

My parents decide to live separately …

_____
_____
_____
_____
_____
_____

My mom loses her job …

_____
_____
_____
_____
_____
_____
_____

Signed:_____ Date:_____

Law and Gospel

The Close of the Commandments
Law and Gospel

God's Good News

That is why I am so eager to preach the gospel also to you who are at Rome. I am not ashamed of the gospel, because it is the power of God for the salvation of everyone who believes: first for the Jew, then for the Gentile. For in the gospel a righteousness from God is revealed, a righteousness that is by faith from first to last, just as it is written: "The righteous will live by faith." Romans 1:15–17

Jason's Story

Jason yawned as he pulled into the church parking lot. He glanced at the dashboard clock: 5:08 a.m. "I didn't know it was so dark at this hour," he thought. He steered the car between the yellow lines. Scrunch! The front tires hit the curb. Jolted by the impact, Jason straightened up in the seat. "I'm glad the curb was there," he muttered, looking around at the other cars.

The Close of the Commandments

What does God say about all these commandments? He says: "I, the Lord your God, am a jealous God, punishing the children for the sin of the fathers to the third and fourth generation of those who hate Me, but showing love to a thousand generations of those who love Me and keep My commandments." [Exodus 20:5–6]

What does this mean? God threatens to punish all who break these commandments. Therefore, we should fear His wrath and not do anything against them. But He promises grace and every blessing to all who keep these commandments. Therefore, we should also love and trust in Him and gladly do what He commands.

The Trinity youth group was hosting a sunrise breakfast at church. Jason was in charge of pancakes. His older sister and brother had always helped with the youth breakfast. They also had made pancakes, and so it was natural that Jason continue the family tradition.

He was running a little late, though. The alarm on his computer desk had shattered the silence at 4:15 a.m., but Jason didn't roll out of bed until 4:35. The bright lights of the bathroom cabinet blinded him at first. Slowly, he had opened his eyes to look in the mirror. Messy hair. A little smudge from last night's outdoor volleyball game. Just enough time for a quick shower.

As Jason walked into the church fellowship hall, his friends were already setting the tables and preparing the main dishes.

"Hey, chef," came a cry from the kitchen area. "We're waiting!"

Jason hurried to join the crew.

"I'm not an expert," he said shyly. "How do we make pancakes, anyway?"

"There's the recipe."

Jason picked up the tattered note card from the counter. "Mix flour, water and eggs in a large bowl. Stir thoroughly. Add other ingredients as desired …," he read aloud. "Well, looks like a good guide to me. Let's get started."

A curb. A mirror. A guide. Simple yet important parts of Jason's day.

How did each object—the curb, the mirror, and the guide (recipe)—benefit Jason?

On first impression, Jason's sunrise breakfast may have little in common with God's Word. But each part—the curb, the mirror, the guide—reveals an important truth about the Law.

God gave the 10 Commandments to reveal His will for His creation. Because of our sinful human nature, it is impossible to obey perfectly His Word. What good, then, is the Law?

Three Purposes

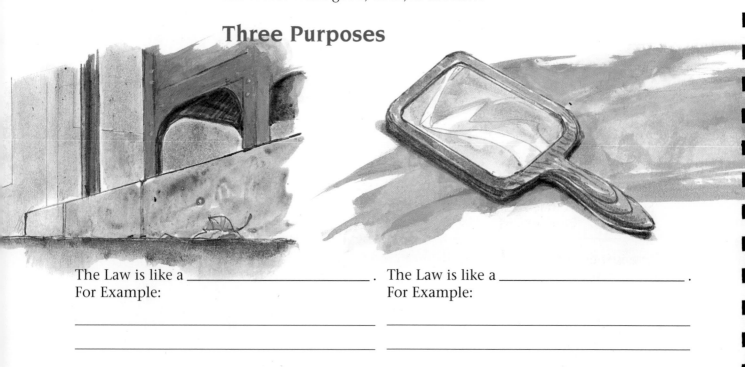

The Law is like a _____ .
For Example:

_____

_____

_____

The Law is like a _____ .
For Example:

_____

_____

_____

The Law is like a _____ .
For Example:

_____

_____

Commandment Identification

Identify each of the following comments according to the commandment to which it most closely applies.

1. "Yes, I turned Bob's employees against him. Why shouldn't I? I don't like Bob." Commandment_____

2. "Most movies use bad language. My friends all swear. It really doesn't matter what I say." Commandment_____

3. "I'm involved in school activities and sports. I have many other commitments. There's really no time for church." Commandment

_____

4. "Nag! Nag! Nag! My parents constantly complain. I get tired of them telling me what I can and cannot do." Commandment

_____

5. "I want what I want. I take what I can. What counts is what I have." Commandment _____

6. "Have you heard the latest about Jenny. I wonder if it's true?" Commandment _____

7. "Sexual intercourse is not wrong when people love each other. It's hard to say 'no.' Some ideals are too 'old-fashioned.' " Commandment

_____

8. "I've just got to have the house and the lifestyle he enjoys. I'm going to do whatever I have to do to get it." Commandment

_____

9. "I know I sometimes put things before God and living for Him. I'm only human." Commandment _____

10. "He hit me and I hit him back." Commandment _____

The Growing Family

- Read the 10 Commandments and explanations for your family devotions. Ask each person first to share a negative example of sin against God's Word. Then, as a family, explore how you may live—in the strength of Christ—a positive witness to each commandment.

- As a family, write on note cards the different ways God is "jealous" for us as His people. Read together "The Close of the Commandments." Offer a prayer that God will work through His Word and sacraments to keep you close in faith and discipleship.

Restoration for Brokenness

• Read the newspaper
together to identify
"Bad News" and "Good
News" in various stories
from around the world.
For the bad news, look
for evidence of human
sinfulness and the reali-
ty of separation, alien-
ation, and hostility. For
the good news, look for
instances of love, kind-
ness, peace, and forgive-
ness. Relate each story
to both the Law and the
Gospel: God's righteous
judgment upon human-
kind and His
undeserved grace—
mercy—in Christ.

• Explain the difference
between Law and
Gospel to your mentor.
Ask him or her to tell
you what the power of
the Gospel has meant in
his or her life.

Therefore, just as sin entered the world through one man, and death through sin, and in this way death came to all men, because all sinned. (Romans 5:12)

For whoever keeps the whole law and yet stumbles at just one point is guilty of breaking all of it. (James 2:10)

Sin is like a ripple. It started with the first man and woman and spread out to all people. Sin is also like knocking over one piece in a domino circle. It affects all other pieces and brings about complete ruin.

Think about the "types" of sin listed below. Write a description, or provide an example, for each category.

Original Sin   Actual Sin   Sins of Commission   Sins of Omission

Human sinfulness carries a stiff penalty: death (Romans 6:23). But in mercy and love, God has paid the price for our sins through the death and resurrection of His Son. In Christ, we hear a second verdict: "Not guilty." Though condemned by our thoughts, words, and deeds, the free, undeserved gift of salvation is ours—by grace, through faith, because of Jesus!

Write a prayer thanking God for showing the love and mercy He has shown you and all people in Jesus.

_____

_____

_____

_____

_____

_____

_____

_____

_____

_____

_____

_____

_____

_____

_____

Signed:_____ Date:_____

11

I Believe

The First Article

One God

For even if there are so-called gods, whether in heaven or on earth (as indeed there are many "gods" and many "lords"), yet for us there is but one God, the Father, from whom all things came and for whom we live; and there is but one Lord, Jesus Christ, through whom all things came and through whom we live. 1 Corinthians 8:5–6

I Believe in God!

"I believe in God." Many people speak these words every day.

Yet for Christians, faith in God is more specific: "I believe in God the Father Almighty, Maker of heaven and earth."

Who is God the Father? In the following column, list 10 words that describe God.

1. forgiving
2. loving
3. honest
4. & fair
5. powerful
6. kind
7. holy
8. Almighty
9. & Creator
10. perfect

The First Article

Creation

I believe in God, the Father Almighty, Maker of heaven and earth.

What does this mean? I believe that God has made me and all creatures; that He has given me my body and soul, eyes, ears, and all my members, my reason and all my senses, and still takes care of them.

He also gives me clothing and shoes, food and drink, house and home, wife and children, land, animals, and all I have. He richly and daily provides me with all that I need to support this body and life.

He defends me against all danger and guards and protects me from all evil.

All this He does only out of fatherly, divine goodness and mercy, without any merit or worthiness in me. For all this it is my duty to thank and praise, serve and obey Him.

This is most certainly true.

A Personal Faith

It was a bright, clear morning. A large crowd had gathered to see the famous Blondin walk across Niagara Falls on a tightrope. Up above, the sun glistened on the surface of the mighty river. Down below, as the torrent of water crashed upon the rocks, a roar like thunder rolled across the valley.

The world's greatest tightrope walker tested the strand that stretched hundreds of feet to the opposite side. He gathered his long pole and, balancing himself expertly, took the first step across the spectacular gorge. The crowd watched in silence. Forward, little by little, Blondin walked the rope. The people on the shore whispered nervously at every sharp movement of the pole. But the great Blondin displayed no fear. Soon he was across, and soon he returned—to the great relief and admiration of the spectators.

Turning to the audience, he made a sensational offer. He would cross the Falls again—this time, though, with a person on his back. Who was willing to go? No one came forward to accept the offer.

Blondin scanned the crowd. "You, sir," he asked, "Do you believe that I am able to carry you across?"

"Yes," came the immediate response.

"Well, then, let's go," Blondin urged.

"Not on your life!" The man quickly disappeared into the crowd.

And so it went. One after another expressed great confidence in the tightrope walker, but no one would agree to let Blondin take him across. Finally, a young fellow moved toward the front of the assembly. Blondin repeated his question. "Do you believe I can carry you across safely?"

"Yes, I do."

"Are you willing to let me?"

"As a matter of fact, I am." The young man, climbed onto the expert's back. Blondin stepped onto the rope, paused momentarily, then walked across the Falls and back with ease.

There were many in that crowd who believed that Blondin could do it. But there was only one who trusted him to do it.

(Taken from *Illustrations for Biblical Preaching,* edited by Michael P. Green, Baker Books, Div. of Baker Book House Co., © 1982, 1985, 1989.)

The story of Blondin demonstrates a great truth about faith. All people know of God from creation, from conscience, or from His Word, the Bible. But not all trust God and His promises!

Faith is trust. Christian faith accepts as true God's Word revealed in the Bible. Christian faith believes the message of God's love and forgiveness shown in the death and resurrection of Jesus. Our Lord and Savior carries us across the canyon of sin and death to heaven—our eternal home! In His mercy, He brings us through all troubles to live with Him forever.

By faith, we know and accept His salvation as certain!

Now faith is being sure of what we hope for and certain of what we do not see. Hebrews 11:1

In what ways is faith like walking over Niagara Falls on the Savior's back?

_____

_____

_____

_____

What words describe faith today?

_____

_____

_____

_____

Ready? Set? Grow!

No one can say, "Jesus is Lord," except by the Holy Spirit.
(1 Corinthians 12:3)

The Growing Family

- Ask your parent[s] for mementos of your faith journey. A Baptismal certificate from the day the Holy Spirit created faith in your heart may be one remembrance. Parents may have kept your first Bible, early Sunday school crafts and lessons, devotional books, or other special gifts. Bring some of these "show and tell" items to the next class.

- Share your creed with your family. Ask parents to sign a note indicating that they have read the creeds and discussed them with you.

With My Mentor

• Ask your mentor to respond to two questions regarding faith. What do you think faith is? What is one word that would describe your faith?

• Ask your mentor, "What are the characteristics that make a person trustworthy?" Explore this idea together, perhaps drawing upon personal illustrations and identifying individuals who have been faithful, dependable friends.

Consequently, faith comes from hearing the message, and the message is heard through the word of Christ. (Romans 10:17)

He saved us, not because of righteous things we had done, but because of His mercy. He saved us through the washing of rebirth and renewal by the Holy Spirit. (Titus 3:5)

"This is My body, which is for you; do this in remembrance of Me. …This cup is the new covenant in My blood; do this, whenever you drink it, in remembrance of Me." (1 Corinthians 11:24–25)

How does faith get in your heart?

_____

_____

My Creed

_____

_____

_____

_____

_____

_____

_____

_____

Signed:_____ Date:_____

12

My Father's World

The First Article

God Takes Care of Us

God blessed Noah and his sons, saying to them, "Be fruitful and increase in number and fill the earth. The fear and dread of you will fall upon all the beasts of the earth and all the birds of the air, upon every creature that moves along the ground, and upon all the fish of the sea; they are given into your hands. Everything that lives and moves will be food for you. Just as I gave you the green plants, I now give you everything." Genesis 9:1–3

On the following lines, list as many of God's good gifts to you as you can, divided among the three categories Luther used in the first three paragraphs of the explanation to the First Article.

All I am _____
body, soul, eyes,
ears, all my members,
reason, and sences
_____
_____
_____
_____

My Life's Essentials and Possessions   Clothing, shoes, food
drink, house, home, wife.   children, land, animals
and all I have
_____

The First Article

Creation

I believe in God the Father Almighty, Maker of heaven and earth.

What does this mean? I believe that God has made me and all creatures; that He has given me my body and soul, eyes, ears, and all my members, my reason and all my senses, and still takes care of them.

He also gives me clothing and shoes, food and drink, house and home, wife and children, land animals, and all I have. He richly and daily provides me with all I need to support this body and life.

He defends me against all danger and guards and protects me from all evil.

All this He does only out of fatherly, divine goodness and mercy, without any merit or worthiness in me. For all this it is my duty to thank and praise, serve and obey Him.

This is most certainly true.

The Good Qualities of My Life _defends me from danger and guards and protects me from evil._

In Hebrews 11 God commends Noah and other Old Testament saints for their faith in His promises. They trusted in God to always take care of them as they lived their lives in the sure and certain knowledge of a better and more complete existence awaiting them in the world to come.

Look up Hebrews 11:13–15. Write in your own words what the saints believed about God's Word.

The saints believed that faithful people were still living by the things promised. Ad

Because of our sinfulness we have deserved none of His goodness toward us. Yet God has blessed us abundantly with all we are and have and have been shown at the hand of our gracious God. Moreover, through Christ God has given us the promise of an eternal home in heaven. While in this world, He gives His forgiven people His Holy Spirit to enable us to live our lives for Him.

Consider each of the following comments about the Christian life. Circle one word to indicate whether you agree or disagree with the statement. Then explain your answer.

a. "Life is tough, and temptations are all around us. I think Christians need to be careful not to enjoy their life here on earth too much."

Agree (Disagree) —————

b. "I am always careful not to become too involved in worldly interests such as human life and environmental concerns. They are political issues. Because of sin, things won't get any better anyway."

Agree (Disagree) —————————

———————————————

———————————————

———————————————

c. "God has blessed me because I have been faithful to Him, plus I am hardworking and dedicated to serving God and others."

Agree (Disagree) —————————

———————————————

———————————————

———————————————

d. "One night I was stranded miles from anywhere on a lonely country road. Out of nowhere a man came down the road in a Cadillac. He fixed my car and then drove away before I could ask him his name. Later I realized that man must have been an angel from God sent to help me."

(Agree) (Disagree) —————————

———————————————

———————————————

———————————————

———————————————

e. "Christians believe what the Bible says about God creating the world because what the Bible teaches about creation is scientifically verifiable."

Agree (Disagree) —————————

———————————————

———————————————

———————————————

The Growing Family

- Invite each member of the family to share an object that represents God's care.

- "The eyes of all look to You, and You give them their food at the proper time. You open Your hand and satisfy the desires of every living thing" (Psalm 145:15–16) is sometimes used as a table prayer. Work together as a family to write your own (original) prayer, thanking God for His many blessings. Make a copy on a note card for each member to pray before and after meals.

49

A Personal Devotion

Read the meditation on the following portion of Acts 17. Pause as directed to apply what you have read to yourself.

"The God who made the world and everything in it is the Lord of heaven and earth and does not live in temples built by hands. And He is not served by human hands, as if He needed anything, because He Himself gives all men life and breath and everything else. From one man He made every nation of men, that they should inhabit the whole earth; (*I am one of these special, unique individuals created by God, who made me along with everything else. My name is* _____ _____) and He determined the times set for them (*my life began on* _____ *at* _____) and the exact places where they should live (*currently I live at* _____). God did this so that men would seek Him and perhaps reach out for Him and find Him, though He is not far from each one of us (*I became a child of God when I was baptized in the name of the Father, Son, and Holy Spirit on* _____ *at* _____ *when* _____ *were my sponsors*). For in Him we live and move and have our being (*Today, I am especially thankful to God for* _____ _____)." Acts 17:24–28a

Signed: _____ Date: _____

With My Mentor

- With your mentor write an inventory of the different ways that you can respect and care for God's creation. Talk with your mentor about stewardship and the various ways we, as the people of God, offer Him our thanks.

- Sin is the source of evil in the world, but God can and does use the bad things that happen in our lives for our good. Read Romans 8:28 together with your mentor. Ask your mentor to recount a difficulty in his or her life that God used for good. With your mentor's permission share your mentor's story at the next class session.

13

Who Is Jesus Christ?

The Second Article

The Word Made Flesh

In the beginning was the Word, and the Word was with God, and the Word was God. He was with God in the beginning. ... The Word became flesh and made His dwelling among us. We have seen His glory, the glory of the One and Only, who came from the Father, full of grace and truth. John 1:1–2, 14

When the time had fully come, God sent His Son, born of a woman, born under law, to redeem those under law, that we might receive the full rights of sons. Galatians 4:4–5

The Second Article

Redemption

[I believe] in Jesus Christ, His only Son, our Lord, who was conceived by the Holy Spirit, born of the Virgin Mary, suffered under Pontius Pilate, was crucified, died and was buried. He descended into hell. The third day He rose again from the dead. He ascended into heaven and sits at the right hand of God, the Father Almighty. From thence He will come to judge the living and the dead.

What does this mean? I believe that Jesus Christ, true God, begotten of the Father from eternity, and also true man, born of the Virgin Mary, is my Lord,

who has redeemed me, a lost and condemned person, purchased and won me from all sins, from death, and from the power of the devil; not with gold or silver, but with His holy, precious blood and with His innocent suffering and death,

that I may be His own and live under Him in His kingdom and serve Him in everlasting righteousness, innocence, and blessedness,

just as He is risen from the dead, lives and reigns to all eternity.

This is most certainly true.

True God, True Man

Divine	Human
unchangeable, present everywhere, eternal almighty, all knowing	thirsty, suffered and died, sleepy, sad was born, hungry

unchangeable, ~~thirsty, suffered and died~~, present everywhere (omnipresent), ~~eternal~~ (without beginning and without end), ~~sleepy~~, ~~sad~~, almighty, was born, hungry, all-knowing (omniscient)

Jesus showed that He was true God and true man. Write the attributes that tell about Jesus' divine nature in the first column. Then write the attributes that tell about His human nature in the second column.

Yes, I Know Him!

He reminds me of other greats like Confucius, Lincoln, and Martin Luther King Jr.

He saved my life. I owe him everything. I want to be more like him every day.

I'd like to know more about him.

He's my competition!

And he's the wisest. I follow his principles, and now I have my act together!

He's the most powerful man I've ever met.

Prophet, Priest, and King

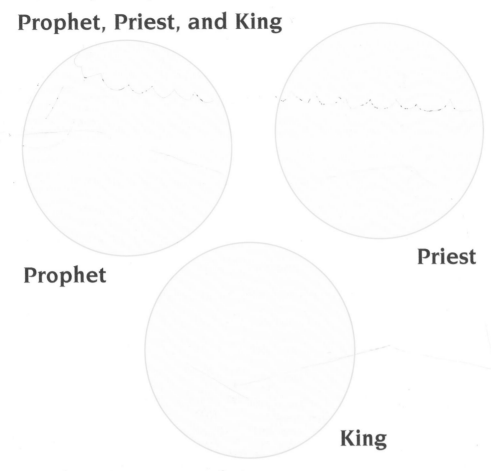

Prophet

Priest

King

I Believe in Jesus Christ

Jinny and Keisha both learned about Portugal. Jinny studied all she could about Portugal and people who are Portuguese. She read about Portugal and studied Portuguese literature, art, and customs. Yet, her life was never really changed because of what she had learned about Portugal.

Keisha never studied Portuguese in school. Keisha and her parents moved and became Portuguese when she was very young. Through the years, she has come to appreciate what it means to be Portuguese because she has grown up among the people of Portugal. Keisha has come to love Portugal and the people of Portugal, the Portuguese.

When I say the words "I believe in Jesus Christ," I mean _____

_____

_____

_____

_____

Signed:_____ Date:_____

The Growing Family

- Discuss with family members what "I believe in Jesus Christ" means to each of you. Then talk about ways to make your faith in Jesus visible in your home. You might consider a Christian picture, motto, or symbol or listening to Christian music on the radio or stereo. Discuss how your faith in Jesus will affect your relationships with other family members.

- Discuss with your family what you would do differently if you could see Jesus in the room with you right now. Remember that Jesus is always with you, the unseen guest at every meal, the unseen listener to every conversation. Discuss how Jesus' presence in your home can affect the way you act and speak to one another.

With My Mentor

- Contact your mentor by phone or in person to talk about what Jesus means to you personally. Ask your mentor how his or her life would be different if he or she didn't know Jesus as Lord and Savior.

- Make a card for your mentors completing the sentence "Jesus Is …," and adding a personal note to your mentor thanking him or her for mentoring you as a brother or sister in Christ.

14

Jesus, My Redeemer

The Second Article

Through Jesus I Am Redeemed

You know that it was not with perishable things such as silver or gold that you were redeemed from the empty way of life handed down to you from your forefathers, but with the precious blood of Christ, a lamb without blemish or defect. 1 Peter 1:18–19

He Himself bore our sins in His body on the tree, so that we might die to sins and live for righteousness; by His wounds you have been healed. 1 Peter 2:24

Introducing ... Jesus

An important out-of-town speaker has consented to make a presentation for your school assembly. You've been asked to introduce Him. As He walks out on the stage, you immediately recognize Him. It's Jesus!

Write your introduction here:

_____

_____

_____

_____

_____

_____

_____

_____

_____

_____

How Humiliating!
Philippians 2:5–8

What Exaltation!
Philippians 2:9–11

In My Place

The heavy cell door clinks shut behind you, and you begin to wonder if your Youth Group's prison visits were such a good idea. "Oh, well," you think, "I only have to stay for 20 minutes. Surely this guy must have something to talk about."

Raul starts in slowly. "I hate this place," he says, "but it's not so bad compared to what I have to look forward to. I killed a guy, you see. Sure, my lawyers are trying to appeal it, but I killed him, and everybody knows I did. My next move from here is death row, and from

Redemption

[I believe] in Jesus Christ, His only Son, our Lord, who was conceived by the Holy Spirit, born of the Virgin Mary, suffered under Pontius Pilate, was crucified, died and was buried. He descended into hell. The third day He rose again from the dead. He ascended into heaven and sits at the right hand of God, the Father Almighty. From thence He will come to judge the living and the dead.

What does this mean? I believe that Jesus Christ, true God, begotten of the Father from eternity, and also true man, born of the Virgin Mary, is my Lord,

who has redeemed me, a lost and condemned person, purchased and won me from all sins, from death, and from the power of the devil; not with gold or silver, but with His holy, precious blood and with His innocent suffering and death

that I may be His own and live under Him in His kingdom and serve Him in everlasting righteousness, innocence, and blessedness,

just as He is risen from the dead, lives and reigns to all eternity.

This is most certainly true.

55

The Growing Family

- As a family project, cut out small cardboard crosses. On each cross write Bible verses or a short sentence that reminds you that Jesus died to take away your sins and make you His children. Carry the cross in your wallet, pocket, or purse as a reminder of whose you are and to whom you belong.

- Because of Jesus' sacrifice for us, we give our lives in service to Him. But often we serve Him best by serving those He has put in families with us. Meditate on the words of Luther's explanation to the Second Article. Then think of one or two ways you can respond to Jesus' love for you by serving someone in your home this week.

With My Mentor

- Write a short note to your mentor explaining how Jesus' redeeming love has changed your life.

- Make something for your mentor that will remind him or her of Jesus' death and resurrection (e.g., a little cross, a picture of a butterfly or Easter lily).

there ... Living is bad enough, thinking every day about what I did. But dying ...

"We tried everything. My lawyers argued and argued. My old man tried to buy off the judge, but money didn't work. Two other guys and I even tried to tunnel out, but the guards caught us, and we got a month in solitary. I'm convinced there's no way out of here.

"I know I deserve the punishment I'm getting. But I'm scared. I would trade places with absolutely anybody in the world. But who would want to take my place—a prisoner with no way out and only certain death ahead?"

What would you say?

_____

_____

_____

_____

Because He Lives

He's Coming Again

On the Last Day, Jesus will return to earth to judge everyone who has ever lived—including you. What will your defense be as you stand before this all-knowing judge?

_____

_____

_____

_____

Signed:_____ Date:_____

56

15

I Believe in the Holy Spirit

The Third Article

Therefore, there is now no condemnation for those who are in Christ Jesus, because through Christ Jesus the law of the Spirit of life set me free from the law of sin and death. Romans 8:1–2 Those who live according to the sinful nature have their minds set on what that nature desires; but those who live in accordance with the Spirit have their minds set on what the Spirit desires. The mind of sinful man is death, but the mind controlled by the Spirit is life and peace. Romans 8:5–6

The Change Agent

"We hired you to be a change agent at Winslow, Inc.," quipped Dane's new boss. "And we are expecting you to help us modernize our office procedures and equipment."

"A change agent," Dane reflected to himself. Twenty-one years old and just out of college, Dane was both excited and worried about the awesome challenge before him as he began his first job. "It's my job to bring about change."

The Holy Spirit is also a change agent. St. Paul in his letter to the Romans describes the working of the Holy Spirit, the greatest possible force for change in any human life. The change the Spirit brings is dynamic, identifiable, and lasting.

What changes does the Holy Spirit work in the lives of God's people?

_____

_____

_____

_____

A New Bo

Bo didn't really like himself much. And he regularly took it out on those around him. A natural leader, Bo often took advantage of the respect others gave him. Bo was a bully. He lied, cheated, and hurt others. Bo sought thrills and satisfaction at every opportunity. Still he wasn't content; his life seemed without meaning or purpose. One day, desperate for a new chance at life, Bo visited a childhood friend. Bo's

The Third Article

Sanctification

I believe in the Holy Spirit, the holy Christian church, the communion of saints, the forgiveness of sins, the resurrection of the body, and the life everlasting. Amen.

What does this mean? I believe that I cannot by my own reason or strength believe in Jesus Christ, my Lord, or come to Him; but the Holy Spirit has called me by the Gospel, enlightened me with His gifts, sanctified and kept me in the true faith.

In the same way He calls, gathers, enlightens, and sanctifies the whole Christian church on earth, and keeps it with Jesus Christ in the one true faith.

In this Christian church He daily and richly forgives all my sins and the sins of all believers.

On the Last Day He will raise me and all the dead, and give eternal life to me and all believers in Christ.

This is most certainly true.

friend told him that Jesus had lived and died a cruel death on the cross to pay for Bo's sins and the sins of all people. Through the words of Bo's friend, the Holy Spirit began working in his life. Sometime later, he confessed Jesus as his Savior and was baptized. Gradually, Bo became a new person. He began to like himself and his actions began to evidence the presence of the Holy Spirit.

Sanctification = the work of the Holy Spirit
Note: The word sanctification is used in two ways:
1. The wide sense: the whole work of the Holy Spirit by which He brings us to faith and also enables us to lead a godly life.
2. The narrow sense: the part of the Holy Spirit's work by which He directs and empowers the believer to lead a godly life.

1. Read Romans 8:1–11. How does Bo's life illustrate the sinful nature and new life according to the Spirit?

_____

_____

2. When did the Holy Spirit "sanctify" Bo in the wide sense of the word?

_____

_____

3. How did the Holy Spirit work in Bo's life according to the narrow meaning of sanctification?

_____

_____

4. According to Romans 8:1–11, why do we need the Holy Spirit to work change in our lives?

_____

_____

How We Grow

The Holy Spirit calls, gathers, enlightens, and sanctifies individual Christians just as He calls, gathers, enlightens, and sanctifies the whole Christian church on earth and keeps it with Jesus Christ in the one true faith.

1. According to Ephesians 4:15, the goal the Holy Spirit desires to bring to us is that …

_____

_____

_____

_____

2. Through the working of the Spirit, the dynamic force at work in the life of the Christian is … (Galatians 5:6)

_____

_____

3. As the Holy Spirit worked in the lives of the early believers who came to faith through Peter's sermon at Pentecost, they … (Acts 2:42)

_____

_____

4. As those who come to know Jesus as their Savior go out into the world, what is the natural result? (Acts 8:4)

_____

_____

5. For what benefit does God make us a church? (Hebrews 10:22–25)

_____

The Growing Family

- Together with your family, read the account of the Philippian jailer and his family coming to faith (Acts 16:23–34). Ask family members to share with each other how faith in Jesus brings joy to their lives. Talk about ways that you can share the joy that comes from knowing Jesus as Lord with other families.

- Ask your parents to tell you about the Holy Spirit's work in your extended family (grandparents, aunts, uncles, cousins). Trace how long the members of your family have believed in Jesus and ask how the working of the Holy Spirit in the lives of ancestors influenced the decisions and goals of their lives. Pray with your family, thanking God for His blessings and faithfulness to your family through the years.

The Story of My Faith

Reflect on the working of the Spirit thus far in your life.

- Interview your mentor, a family member, or another adult, about their faith in Jesus. Ask questions such as, "What were you like before becoming a Christian?" "How did you become different?" "Did you change quickly?" "Has it always been easy?" "Have you ever felt like a failure as a Christian? What else could you tell us about that?" "What difference do you think it makes in your life now?" "Where do you think you will be in your Christian faith a couple years from now?"

- Think about the ways that the Holy Spirit has worked—and is still working—in the life of this person to create and sustain faith in our Savior-Lord.

- Discuss with your mentor the words of a favorite hymn that focuses on the person and work of the Holy Spirit. Look in your congregation's hymnal for suggestions. Ask your mentor to help explain each stanza and talk about how the meaning of the stanzas applies to our lives and the world around us.

1. The beginning of my faith, when I first became a Christian, or my earliest memory of being a Christian:

_____

_____

_____

2. My favorite time at church, or being with Christians, is …

_____

_____

_____

3. The person who most reminds me of Jesus is …

_____

_____

_____

She/he reminds me of Jesus because …

_____

_____

_____

4. One incident from my life that speaks clearly to me about my relationship with Jesus:

_____

_____

5. What I now believe, or how I live as a Christian:

_____

_____

_____

_____

_____

_____

_____

Signed:_____ Date:_____

16

A New Me!

The Third Article

A New Beginning

What shall we say, then? Shall we go on sinning so that grace may increase? By no means! We died to sin; how can we live in it any longer? Or don't you know that all of us who were baptized into Christ Jesus were baptized into His death? We were therefore buried with Him through baptism into death in order that, just as Christ was raised from the dead through the glory of the Father, we too may live a new life.

If we have been united with Him like this in His death, we will certainly also be united with Him in His resurrection. For we know that our old self was crucified with Him so that the body of sin might be done away with, that we should no longer be slaves to sin—because anyone who has died has been freed from sin.

Now if we died with Christ, we believe that we will also live with Him.

Romans 6:1–8

1. How is it possible for a just and holy God to declare sinners righteous (justification)?

because Jesus died to save us from our sins

2. Why is it crucial that we firmly hold to the teaching of justification by grace, for Christ's sake, through faith?

a. He will watch over us.

b. Distingueses the critian religion by fake religion

c. Gives us enduring comfort to sinners

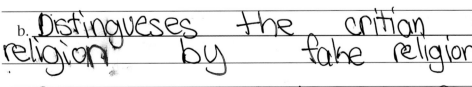

The Third Article

I believe in … the forgiveness of sins, the resurrection of the body, and the life everlasting. Amen.

What does this mean? … In this Christian church He daily and richly forgives all my sins and the sins of all believers. On the Last Day He will raise me and all the dead, and give eternal life to me and all believers in Christ. This is most certainly true.

Before and After

Before

1. Write a brief story to accompany these *before* and *after* pictures.

_____

_____

_____

_____

_____

_____

2. Explain how the work of the Holy Spirit make us new people in Christ.

_____

_____

_____

_____

_____

_____

62

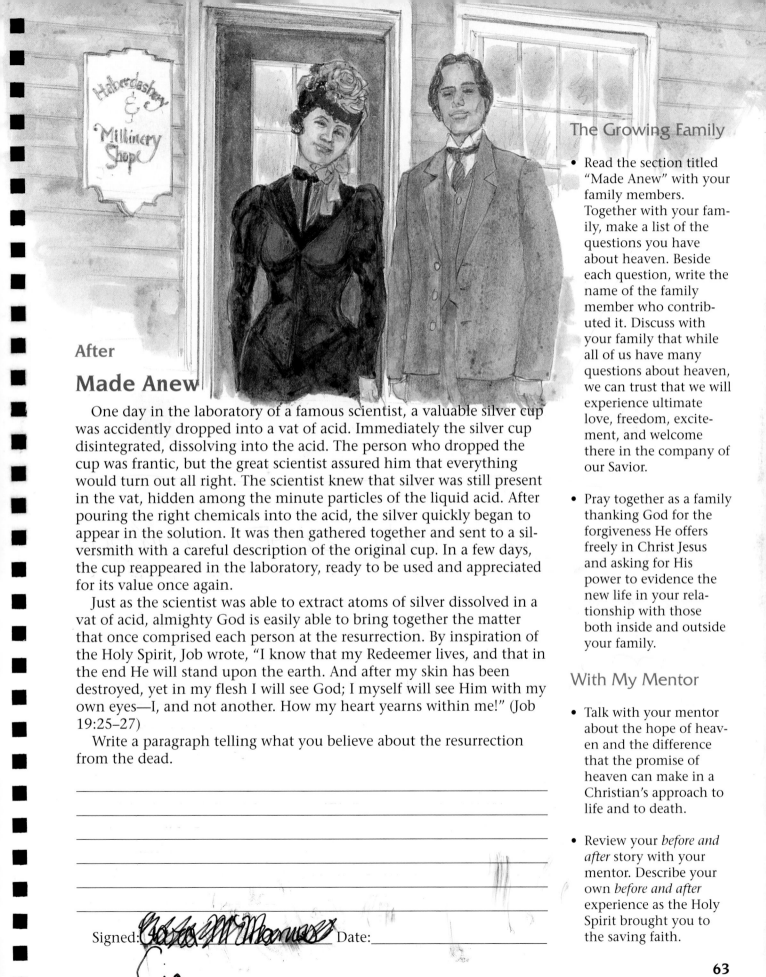

After

Made Anew

One day in the laboratory of a famous scientist, a valuable silver cup was accidently dropped into a vat of acid. Immediately the silver cup disintegrated, dissolving into the acid. The person who dropped the cup was frantic, but the great scientist assured him that everything would turn out all right. The scientist knew that silver was still present in the vat, hidden among the minute particles of the liquid acid. After pouring the right chemicals into the acid, the silver quickly began to appear in the solution. It was then gathered together and sent to a silversmith with a careful description of the original cup. In a few days, the cup reappeared in the laboratory, ready to be used and appreciated for its value once again.

Just as the scientist was able to extract atoms of silver dissolved in a vat of acid, almighty God is easily able to bring together the matter that once comprised each person at the resurrection. By inspiration of the Holy Spirit, Job wrote, "I know that my Redeemer lives, and that in the end He will stand upon the earth. And after my skin has been destroyed, yet in my flesh I will see God; I myself will see Him with my own eyes—I, and not another. How my heart yearns within me!" (Job 19:25–27)

Write a paragraph telling what you believe about the resurrection from the dead.

_____

_____

_____

_____

_____

_____

Signed: _____ Date: _____

The Growing Family

- Read the section titled "Made Anew" with your family members. Together with your family, make a list of the questions you have about heaven. Beside each question, write the name of the family member who contributed it. Discuss with your family that while all of us have many questions about heaven, we can trust that we will experience ultimate love, freedom, excitement, and welcome there in the company of our Savior.

- Pray together as a family thanking God for the forgiveness He offers freely in Christ Jesus and asking for His power to evidence the new life in your relationship with those both inside and outside your family.

With My Mentor

- Talk with your mentor about the hope of heaven and the difference that the promise of heaven can make in a Christian's approach to life and to death.

- Review your *before and after* story with your mentor. Describe your own *before and after* experience as the Holy Spirit brought you to the saving faith.

17

Joined by Prayer: Anytime, Anywhere

Prayer

How to Pray

Then Jesus told His disciples a parable to show them that they should always pray and not give up. He said: "In a certain town there was a judge who neither feared God nor cared about men. And there was a widow in that town who kept coming to him with the plea, 'Grant me justice against my adversary.'

"For some time he refused. But finally he said to himself, 'Even though I don't fear God or care about men, yet because this widow keeps bothering me, I will see that she gets justice, so that she won't eventually wear me out with her coming!'"

And the Lord said, "Listen to what the unjust judge says. And will not God bring about justice for His chosen ones, who cry out to Him day and night? Will He keep putting them off? I tell you, He will see that they get justice, and quickly. However, when the Son of Man comes, will He find faith on the earth?" Luke 18:1–8

What a friend we have in Jesus,
All our sins and griefs to bear!
What a privilege to carry
Ev'rything to God in prayer!
Oh, what peace we often forfeit;
Oh what needless pain we bear—
All because we do not carry
Ev'rything to God in prayer!

A S K

Ask and it will be given to you;
Seek and you will find;
Knock and the door will be opened to you.
For everyone who asks receives; he who seeks finds; and to him who knocks, the door will be opened. Matthew 7:7–8

Prayer Fishbone

Prayer	to whom?	what?	where?	when?	how?

The Prayer Jesus Taught Us

My Prayer Journal

_____

_____

_____

_____

Our Father who art in heaven.

_____

Hallowed be Thy name.

_____

Thy kingdom come, Thy will be done, on earth as it is in heaven.

_____

_____

Give us this day our daily bread.

_____

_____

And forgive us our trespasses as we forgive those who trespass against us.

_____

_____

Lead us not into temptation.

_____

_____

But deliver us from evil.

_____

_____

For Thine is the kingdom and the power and the glory forever and ever.

_____

The Growing Family

- God encourages prayer everywhere. Prayer is always appropriate in one's own family. Give each member of your family one sheet of paper. Tell them to fold the sheet into thirds so it will stand up. On one side of their sheet, ask each person to list prayer concerns which are *common* to most families. On the second side, direct them to list specific prayer concerns *unique* to your family. On the third side, have them list prayer concerns which they *personally* have right *now*. These written prayer lists are helpful to remember prayer concerns as you and your family pray for each other daily. Some members of your family might want to write personal prayers, requests, or thanksgivings on the card. A younger brother or sister who is too young to write a prayer card, could participate by decorating the card with pictures of things your family prays for regularly.

- Ask older members of your extended family, such as grandparents, to share prayers, especially in another language, that they may recall from their childhood. This can be especially fun to do at larger family gatherings and at mealtime during special celebrations or holidays. Write down and try to memorize at least one "traditional" family prayer that you did not know before and share it with the class the next time you meet.

With My Mentor

- Ask your mentor to share what prayer means to him or her, interesting prayer customs they may have, and *times* and *places* for prayer that are or have been special to them. Jesus' promises in Matthew 18:20 "where two or three come together in my name," and Matthew 18:19 "if two of you on earth agree about anything you ask for ..." direct us to pray regularly with others.

- Pray with your mentor. Talk about *why* it is important to know that someone else is praying for you each day.

Amen.

_____

_____

God's Word on Prayer

According to His will

_____

_____

In the name of Jesus

_____

_____

Praying with confidence

_____

_____

Regular and frequent prayer

_____

_____

The Acts of Prayer

Prayer is ...
Adoration

_____

_____

Confession

_____

_____

Thanksgiving

_____

_____

Supplication

_____

_____

Signed:_____ Date:_____

18

Prayer: A Conversation with the Father

The Lord's Prayer
The Introduction
The First Petition

Good Gifts

Which of you fathers, if your son asks for a fish, will give him a snake instead? Or if he asks for an egg, will give him a scorpion? If you then, though you are evil, know how to give good gifts to your children, how much more will your Father in heaven give the Holy Spirit to those who ask Him! Luke 11:11–13

The City of Everywhere

There's a story told by High Price Hughes called "The City of Everywhere." A man arrives at a train station one wintry day, hails a cab, and notices something peculiar: the driver is barefooted.

"Pardon me," the man says as he slides into the back seat. "I'm curious why you don't wear shoes. Don't you believe in them?"

The Introduction

Our Father who art in heaven.

Our Father in heaven.

What does this mean? With these words God tenderly invites us to believe that He is our true Father and that we are His true children, so that with all boldness and confidence we may ask Him as dear children ask their dear father.

The First Petition

Hallowed be Thy name.

Hallowed be Your name.

What does this mean? God's name is certainly holy in itself, but we pray in this petition that it may be kept holy among us also.

How is God's name kept holy? God's name is kept holy when the Word of God is taught in its truth and purity, and we, as the children of God, also lead holy lives according to it. Help us to do this, dear Father in heaven! But anyone who teaches or lives contrary to God's Word profanes the name of God among us. Protect us from this, heavenly Father!

The Growing Family

- Just as a family name is special, God's name is special. Perhaps some within your family has had their name misused in a joke or a rhyme. Talk about how that feels, and how God feels when we don't use His name in prayer. How do you *feel* when you hear someone else misuse God's name?

- Talk about ways that God's name is hallowed, and not hallowed in your family. Everyone may misuse God's name, but many people don't talk about it. Talk about your shame and guilt at misusing God's name, and agree to encourage each other with the forgiveness we have in Christ Jesus.

"Sure," says the driver.

"Then why don't you wear them?"

The driver replies, "Ah, that's the question." Why don't we? Why don't we?"

Later, outside a restaurant, the man notices that everyone in the town is walking barefooted in the snow. He stops a passerby to ask again about shoes. After all it is winter!

"Don't you see how my shoes protect my feet?"

"Well, sure I do," replies the passerby. "See that building over there? That's a shoe factory. We go there every week to hear the manager tell us how wonderful shoes are. We're mighty proud of our shoe factory."

"Then, why aren't you wearing shoes?"

"Ah, that's the question. Why don't we? Why don't we? In the same way, we can know all about prayer. So why don't we do it?"

(Adapted from *Teachers Interaction*, "Teaching Children to Pray," by Julaine Kammrath, June 1994, p. 25. Used by permission.)

Picture This ... God Is My Father!

Consider the following pictures. Of which attributes of your heavenly Father do the men in these pictures remind you?

- Encourage older family members, parents, and especially grandparents to recall prayer times and prayer habits within their families.

With My Mentor

- Ask your mentor to recall his/her earliest recollections of praying the Lord's Prayer. Talk about different places where the Lord's Prayer is used— regularly in church, at weddings, funerals, and other public services. How do you feel about the argument that if used too often, the Lord's Prayer will become meaningless— compare eating three meals a day and not growing tired of food. Explore with your mentor ways to keep your *use* of the Lord's Prayer fresh and exciting.

- With your mentor discuss the connection between the First Petition of the Lord's Prayer and the Second Commandment, "Don't use God's name in vain, but use it in prayer, praise, and thanksgiving."

Persons I Will Pray For

Name	I will ask God to ...

Signed:_____ Date:_____

19

Captured in the Cross

The Lord's Prayer
The Second Petition
The Third Petition

By Grace Alone

For it is by grace you have been saved, through faith—and this not from yourselves, it is the gift of God—not by works, so that no one can boast. Ephesians 2:8–9

Playing on the Team

It's "Dream Team" history for kids around the United States. Several Major League coaches have decided to put together teams of youth from their respective areas to play in a national tournament in St. Louis. Ricardo lives in Chicago, and would love to play on the youth Cubs team when it goes to the tournament. He knows that each Major League coach has assigned other coaches to select the players and equip them for the games.

How does entry into this youth tournamment *contrast* with our entry into God's Kingdom?

_____
_____
_____
_____
_____
_____
_____

God's Kingdoms

There are three great kingdoms within the domain of God. His kingdom of power displays total control of all things in heaven and on earth. God is not only the Maker of all things material and spiritual, He is also the one who keeps them in existence. The kingdom of power includes all that is within His creative and sustaining will.

The kingdom of grace is what is revealed in the work of Jesus Christ. John says it like this."For the law was given through Moses; grace and truth came through Jesus Christ" (John 1:17). The knowledge of God's grace, His love for each and every person, is not known through the things of creation. God has given this knowledge to believers. The kingdom of grace is witnessed within the faithful church.

The last kingdom is the kingdom of glory. This is God's kingdom as it is witnessed beyond the powers of the devil, the world, and our sinful nature. It is God dwelling with all His angels and the saints in heaven. It is the kingdom of perfection, where nothing evil exists.

Decide which kingdom is represented in the following and write it in the correct box.

Saints standing before God's throne in heaven

A sinner's sin being forgiven

People hearing of God's love

A beautiful sunset

Picture of stars in dark sky

Jesus at the right hand of God's throne

People attending Holy Communion

Large waves striking a beach

A baby being baptized

A nuclear generator

Artist's picture of a heavenly banquet

Kingdom of Power	Kingdom of Grace	Kingdom of Glory

The Second Petition

Thy kingdom come.

Your kingdom come.

What does this mean? The kingdom of God certainly comes by itself without our prayer, but we pray in this petition that it may come to us also.

How does God's kingdom come? God's kingdom comes when our heavenly Father gives us His Holy Spirit, so that by His grace we believe His holy Word and lead godly lives here in time and there in eternity.

The Third Petition

Thy will be done on earth as it is in heaven.

Your will be done on earth as in heaven.

What does this mean? The good and gracious will of God is done even without our prayer, but we pray in this petition that it may be done among us also.

How is God's will done? God's will is done when He breaks and hinders every evil plan and purpose of the devil, the world, and our sinful nature, which do not want us to hallow God's name or let His kingdom come; and when He strengthens and keeps us firm in His Word and faith until we die. This is His good and gracious will.

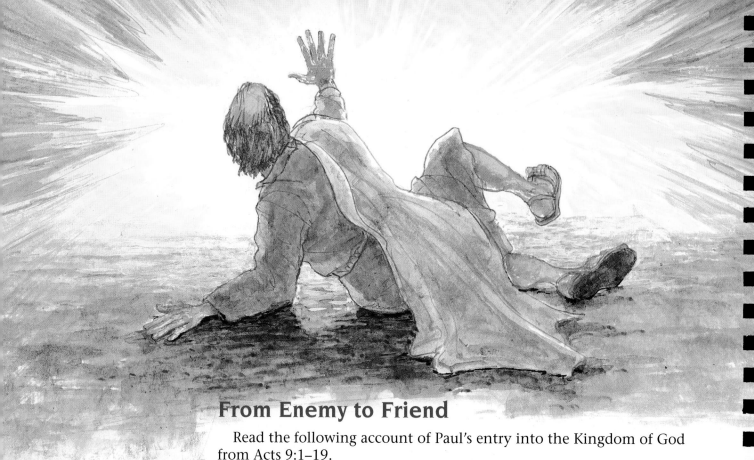

From Enemy to Friend

Read the following account of Paul's entry into the Kingdom of God from Acts 9:1–19.

Reader 1: Meanwhile, Saul was still breathing out murderous threats against the Lord's disciples. He went to the high priest and asked him for letters to the synagogues in Damascus, so that if he found any there who belonged to the Way, whether men or women, he might take them as prisoners to Jerusalem. As he neared Damascus on his journey, suddenly a light from heaven flashed around him. He fell to the ground and heard a voice say to him,

Reader 2: "Saul, Saul, why do you persecute Me?"

Reader 3: "Who are You, Lord?"

Reader 2: "I am Jesus, whom you are persecuting. Now get up and go into the city, and you will be told what you must do."

Reader 1: The men traveling with Saul stood there speechless; they heard the sound but did not see anyone. Saul got up from the ground, but when he opened his eyes he could see nothing. So they led him by the hand into Damascus. For three days he was blind, and did not eat or drink anything. In Damascus there was a disciple named Ananias. The Lord called to him in a vision,

Reader 2: "Ananias!"

Reader 4: "Yes, Lord."

Reader 1: The Lord told him,

Reader 2: "Go to the house of Judas on Straight Street and ask for a man from Tarsus named Saul, for he is praying. In a vision he has seen a man named Ananias come and place his hands on him to restore his sight."

Reader 1: Ananias answered,

The Growing Family

- God works in the lives of His people to extend and hasten the coming of His kingdom. Read and discuss these Bible passages with your parents and other members of your family: Mark 1:15, Matt. 13:31–33, 1 Cor. 4:20. Apply the message of these verses to the extending of God's kingdom of grace.

- Build a domino chain with your family. You could make it a straight line or build it with elaborate bends and curves. When completed, ask the youngest family member to push over the first domino and then watch the chain reaction. If the chain is successful, all the dominos will fall with the first.

Reader 4: "Lord, I have heard many reports about this man and all the harm he has done to Your saints in Jerusalem. And he has come here with authority from the chief priests to arrest all who call on Your name."

Reader 1: But the Lord said to Ananias,

Reader 2: "Go! This man is My chosen instrument to carry My name before the Gentiles and their kings and before the people of Israel. I will show him how much he must suffer for My name."

Reader 1: Then Ananias went to the house and entered it. Placing his hands on Saul, he said,

Reader 4: "Brother Saul, the Lord—Jesus, who appeared to you on the road as you were coming here—has sent me so that you may see again and be filled with the Holy Spirit."

Reader 1: Immediately, something like scales fell from Saul's eyes, and he could see again. He got up and was baptized, and after taking some food, he regained his strength. Saul spent several days with the disciples in Damascus.

Write your responses to the following:

1. How did Paul enter God's kingdom of grace?

_____

_____

2. When are we like Ananias who at first was unwilling to serve, as God's kingdom of grace reached for Paul?

_____

_____

3. Paul's Baptism is a sign of which kingdom of God?

_____

_____

4. On the lines below write a brief statement explaining what each of the three kingdoms means to you.

Kingdom of power ———————————————

_____

Kingdom of grace ————————————————

_____

Kingdom of glory ————————————————

_____

_____

Signed:_____ Date:_____

• The faith we have today is the result of Christ's action on the cross—represented by the first domino. It was communicated by the power of the Holy Spirit, through the community of faith, to each of the family members. God now seeks to use each of the family members, as they form His kingdom of grace in the world, to bring others by His Spirit into His eternal family.

• Read as a family Hebrews 12:1–3. Note how the Scripture points to Christ as the "author and perfecter" of our faith, and that this faith has been communicated through a "great cloud of witnesses." Finally, each person is encouraged to join in with that "great cloud," set their eyes upon Jesus, and avoid anything that would hinder the kingdom of grace within our lives.

With My Mentor

• Interview one or more mentors, asking these two questions: Who in your life most influenced your faith in Jesus Christ? What about this person most particularly impacted your faith?

• Talk with your mentor about a portion of God's Word that is a favorite of his or hers.

20

Our Daily Bread

The Lord's Prayer
The Fourth Petition

No Way

Seek first His kingdom and His righteousness, and all these things will be given to you as well. Therefore do not worry about tomorrow, for tomorrow will worry about itself. Each day has enough trouble of its own. Matthew 6:33–34

Just Imagine

What would you do if someone gave you $1,000? Let's cut that amount down. What if someone gave you $200? How would you spend a *mere* $200? On the following lines, write down everything you would do with $200.

_____

_____

_____

_____

_____

_____

In many third world countries, $200 is the *average* income of a family—for an entire year! The sum of $200, just imagine! Even the most careful of shoppers would find it *very* hard to make $200 cover the monthly food bill for a typical family in America. We take so much for granted. Fine foods, comfortable houses, lively recreation. As Americans, we kind of just expect to have good things.

In what ways do you take for granted what you've been given?

_____

_____

_____

Maybe you've seen it—a woman sitting on the corner, holding a sign. Written in charcoal, the sign reads "Hungry, will work for food. God bless you!" She hopes you will stop your car and give her some money. Or you see a man, dirty, dressed in military fatigues, pushing a grocery cart full of an odd assortment of bottles, papers, an old umbrella. A mangy, malnourished dog walks beside him. When you see people in this condition, what do you think?

_____

_____

How do you react?

_____

_____

Let Us Thank Him

Give us this day our daily bread.

Give us today our daily bread.

What does this mean? God certainly gives daily bread to everyone without our prayers, even to all evil people, but we pray in this petition that God would lead us to realize this and to receive our daily bread with thanksgiving.

What is meant by daily bread? Daily bread includes everything that has to do with the support and needs of the body, such as food, drink, clothing, shoes, house, home, land, animals, money, goods, a devout husband or wife, devout children, devout workers, devout and faithful rulers, good government, good weather, peace, health, self control, good reputation, good friends, faithful neighbors, and the like.

Read Acts 3:1–10 and answer the questions below.

1. What physical problems did the man have?

_____

_____

75

2. What did he want from Peter and John?

_____

_____

3. What did he get?

_____

_____

4. How did the man respond?

_____

_____

5. Compare the man's request with what he received. How does what we have received from God compare with what we deserve?

_____

_____

6. What do each of the following passages say about how by the power of the Holy Spirit God's people are moved to respond to Him for the many blessings He has given us?

_____

_____

    a. Hebrews 13:16

_____

_____

    b. 1 John 3:17–18

_____

_____

    c. Acts 20:35

_____

_____

The Growing Family

- On a smaller scale, families can experience the joy of giving to others while experiencing hunger. Once or twice a month, skip a main meal (fast) in order to help you and your family focus on what God has done for you in Christ. At meal time substitute devotions, songs, family games, and discussions. Commit the money saved to help someone else. If every family skipped two meals a month enough money would likely be generated to support a child in a third world country. Giving to others is an excellent way to demonstrate joy and appreciation to God for all He has given us through Christ Jesus our Lord.

- If the common table prayer has become "old hat" to your family, do something about it! Help your family make thanksgiving a daily, fresh part of your lives. Work together as a family to write a new table prayer. Share with your family the things you are thankful for and ask family members to share things they are thankful for with you. Share your new prayer with the class at your next meeting.

A Grateful Response

Consider *everything* you've been given! If you're like most American teenagers, you have to admit that you've been blessed! We pray "give us this day our daily bread," and God in His mercy gives us so many things. On the space on the next page, list everything you're thankful for. Write one blessing that you are especially grateful for today on each of the loaves of bread. If you get stuck, look at "What is meant by daily bread?"

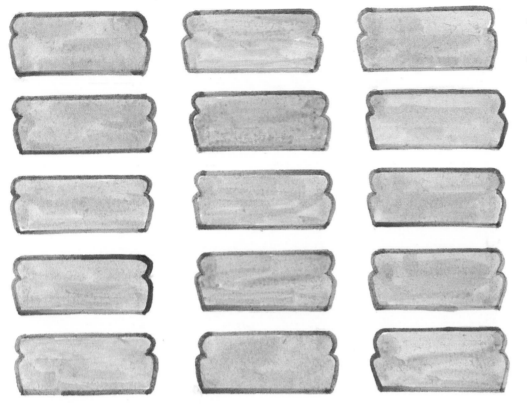

Praise God He does not treat us the way we *deserve* to be treated! Instead of the eternal punishment and death that would be ours because of sin, God gives us life! He gives us everything we have—including Jesus whom He sent in order to make us God's own. He gives us the Holy Spirit to empower us to new life.

Through your Baptism God calls you His child. Further, He gives you the Holy Spirit to empower you to be a servant for Him. What is God calling you to do as a result of what you have studied in this lesson? In the space below write down as many things you can think of that represent things you can do *now* to serve the Lord. Talk about them with your classmates, teachers, parents, and mentors. Commit yourself to doing at least one of these this year.

_____

_____

_____

_____

_____

_____

_____

_____

Signed:_____ Date:_____

With My Mentor

- One of the greatest gifts God has given us is the gift of His Son, Jesus. Every time we celebrate the Sacrament of the Altar, we cherish this gift given so freely to us. Ask your mentor to work with you to provide communion bread for your congregation's celebration of Holy Communion. You can find recipes for unleavened bread in many Jewish cookbooks, which can be checked out from your local library. Gather ingredients and set aside time to work with your mentor on this project. As you work together, discuss thankfulness, the meaning of Passover, and the Sacrament.

- Make plans with your mentor to visit a soup kitchen, retirement home, state home, or other agency where the services provided have a significant impact in the lives of others.

21

Forgiveness Is for Giving

The Lord's Prayer
The Fifth Petition

The Power of Forgiveness

"I tell you, whatever you ask for in prayer, believe that you have received it, and it will be yours. And when you stand praying, if you hold anything against anyone, forgive him, so that your Father in heaven may forgive you your sins." Mark 11:24–25

The Fifth Petition

And forgive us our trespasses as we forgive those who trespass against us.

Forgive us our sins as we forgive those who sin against us.

What does this mean? We pray in this petition that our Father in heaven would not look at our sins, or deny our prayer because of them. We are neither worthy of the things for which we pray, nor have we deserved them, but we ask that He would give them all to us by grace, for we daily sin much and surely deserve nothing but punishment. So we too will sincerely forgive and gladly do good to those who sin against us.

Who's Forgiveness for Anyway?

Juan, Philipe, Maria, and Alice were seated at the lunch table. "I just don't understand that religion lesson today," said Maria. "Mr. Hernandez said that we should forgive everyone, just like Jesus did. But I don't know if I'll ever forgive Georgina. She told my secret after she promised never to say anything to anyone. Now everyone keeps making fun of me. I'm so mad, I don't think I'll ever talk to her again."

"But Mr. Hernandez said that Jesus loves everybody, even His enemies and that we're supposed to do the same," chimed in Alice.

"Well, that sounds nice," said Maria, "but it just doesn't work in real life. Jesus never met anyone as nasty as Georgina. I hate her. I suppose maybe I could forgive her some day if she did something to make up for what she did wrong—but not until then!"

"But Mr. Hernandez said that forgiveness is free. That we should forgive just like Jesus did, even when you don't feel like it."

"No way," said Maria. "I think you have to earn forgiveness, to do something to show you're worthy of it."

Juan added, "Yeah. I think Maria's right. And I'm not so sure Jesus forgives everyone anyway. We read in history class about how Hitler killed six million Jews. Could God forgive people like that?"

"And what about those people we heard about on the news?" said Philipe, "like the woman who abused her children, or the guy caught selling drugs at the school down the street. How could Jesus forgive people like that? Aren't some sins just too bad to forgive?"

For Reflection

1. Are some sins so bad they can't be forgiven? _____
2. What does the Bible say (John 3:16; 1 John 1:6–8)?

He had no beauty or majesty to attract us to Him, nothing in His appearance that we should desire Him. He was despised and rejected by men, a man of sorrows, and familiar with suffering. Like one from whom men hide their faces He was despised, and we esteemed Him not. Surely He took up our infirmities and carried our sorrows, yet we considered Him stricken by God, smitten by Him, and afflicted. But He was pierced for our transgressions, He was crushed for our iniquities; the punishment that brought us peace was upon Him, and by His wounds we are healed. Isaiah 53:2–5

Then the governor's soldiers took Jesus into the Praetorium and gathered the whole company of soldiers around Him. They stripped Him and put a scarlet robe on Him, and then twisted together a crown of thorns and set it on His head. They put a staff in His right hand and knelt in front of Him and mocked Him. "Hail, king of the Jews!" they said. They spit on Him, and took the staff and struck Him on the head again and again. After they had mocked Him, they took off the robe and put His own clothes on Him. Then they led Him away to crucify Him. Matthew 27:27–31

From the sixth hour until the ninth hour darkness came over all the land. About the ninth hour Jesus cried out in a loud voice, *"Eloi, Eloi, lama sabachthani?"*—which means, "My God, my God, why have you forsaken me?" Matthew 27:45–46

The Growing Family

- Make a list of your troubles and describe how forgiveness gets at each one.

- Set aside 10 minutes at the end of the week for "Reconciliation Time." Talk about things that are bothering you at home, at school, or at work. Listen to each other. Close with a prayer asking for God's power to forgive, or have each person speak a one-sentence prayer about forgiveness.

- Read Bible stories of forgiveness (e.g., Genesis 50:15–21 and Matthew 18:23–35). Do one of the following together as a family: (1) act out the story, (2) retell the story with a modern situation, (3) draw a picture (or do a finger painting) illustrating the point of the story and hang it on the refrigerator, (4) rewrite the story as a poem or a "rap" and then perform it as a family.

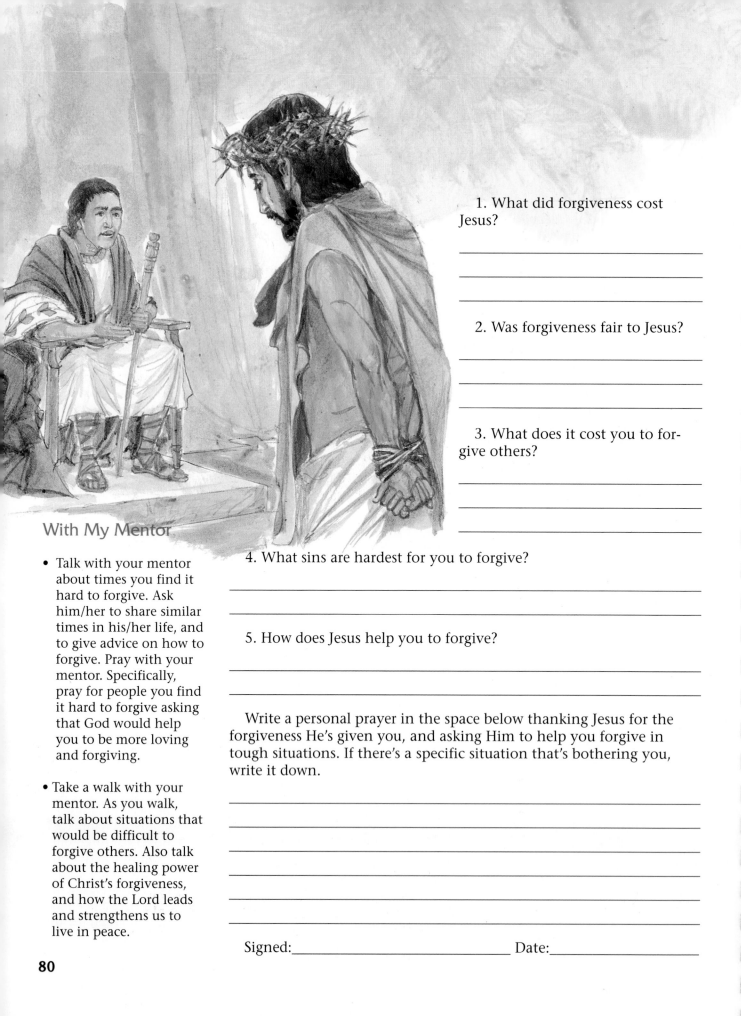

1. What did forgiveness cost Jesus?

_____

_____

_____

2. Was forgiveness fair to Jesus?

_____

_____

_____

3. What does it cost you to forgive others?

_____

_____

_____

With My Mentor

- Talk with your mentor about times you find it hard to forgive. Ask him/her to share similar times in his/her life, and to give advice on how to forgive. Pray with your mentor. Specifically, pray for people you find it hard to forgive asking that God would help you to be more loving and forgiving.

- Take a walk with your mentor. As you walk, talk about situations that would be difficult to forgive others. Also talk about the healing power of Christ's forgiveness, and how the Lord leads and strengthens us to live in peace.

4. What sins are hardest for you to forgive?

_____

_____

5. How does Jesus help you to forgive?

_____

_____

Write a personal prayer in the space below thanking Jesus for the forgiveness He's given you, and asking Him to help you forgive in tough situations. If there's a specific situation that's bothering you, write it down.

_____

_____

_____

_____

_____

_____

Signed:_____ Date:_____

80

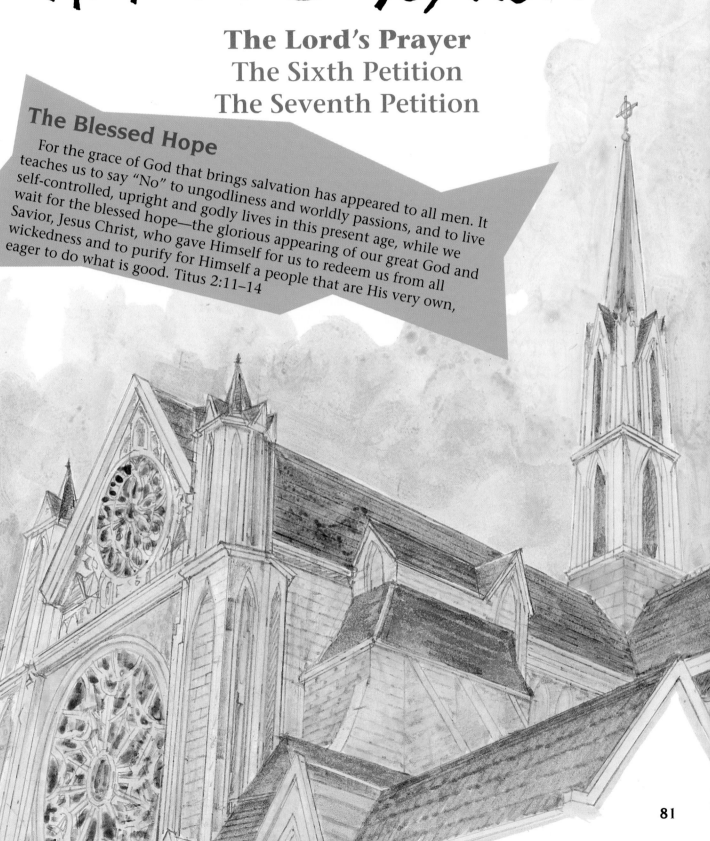

22

Keep Us Safe, Lord!

The Lord's Prayer
The Sixth Petition
The Seventh Petition

The Blessed Hope

For the grace of God that brings salvation has appeared to all men. It teaches us to say "No" to ungodliness and worldly passions, and to live self-controlled, upright and godly lives in this present age, while we wait for the blessed hope—the glorious appearing of our great God and Savior, Jesus Christ, who gave Himself for us to redeem us from all wickedness and to purify for Himself a people that are His very own, eager to do what is good. Titus 2:11–14

One Little Word

Martin Luther, bold and strong in his faith, thought much about temptation and the power of what he called the unholy trinity—the devil, the world, and our sinful nature. In his famous hymn, "A Mighty Fortress Is Our God," Luther wrote about the power of God to help us in the ongoing battle against all that wages war against our saving faith in Christ. Luther wrote,

> A mighty fortress is our God, A trusty shield and weapon;
> He helps us free from ev'ry need That hath us now o'ertaken,
> The old evil foe Now means deadly woe;
> Deep guile and great might Are his dread arms in fight;
> On earth is not his equal.

> With might of ours can naught be done, Soon were our loss effected;
> But for us fights the valiant One, Whom God Himself elected.
> Ask ye, Who is this? Jesus Christ it is,
> Of sabaoth Lord, and there's none other God;
> He holds the field forever.

> Though devils all the world should fill, All eager to devour us,
> We tremble not, we fear no ill, They shall not overpower us.
> This world's prince may still Scowl fierce as he will,
> He can harm us none, He's judged; the deed is done;
> One little word can fell him.

> The Word they still shall let remain Nor any thanks have for it;
> He's by our side upon the plain With His good gifts and Spirit.
> And take they our life, Goods, fame, child, and wife,
> Though these all be gone, Our victory has been won;
> The kingdom ours remaineth.

1. Whom did Luther call "this world's prince"?

_____

2. What "one little word" can fell the world's prince?

_____

_____

_____

3. Circle each group of words in the hymn that refers to the forces of evil that seek to undermine the Christian in his or her life of faith. Underline each group of words in the hymn that tells of God's action on our behalf and the blessings He gives us.

In the Battle

Consider each of the following scenarios. Identify the harmful force or element in each situation. Then give one way that, by the Spirit's power, we could give God glory in each situation.

1. Sharla's new friends are inviting her to go to a party at the home of some high schoolers whose parents are out of town for the weekend. She knows there will be drinking and drugs at the party.

_____

_____

The Sixth Petition

And lead us not into temptation.

Lead us not into temptation.

What does this mean? God tempts no one. We pray in this petition that God would guard and keep us so that the devil, the world, and our sinful nature may not deceive us or mislead us into false belief, despair, and other great shame and vice. Although we are attacked by these things, we pray that we may finally overcome them and win the victory.

82

2. Bill and Ellie are on their first date when it becomes apparent to Bill that Ellie expects him to have sex with her.

_____

_____

3. Bruce is spending the weekend with Mike Harris and his family. On Sunday the Harris' invite Bruce to attend their church with them. The Harris family belongs to a church that does not believe Jesus is God's Son and the Savior of the world.

_____

_____

4. Jacquie and her family are active members of their church. When Jacquie discovers she is pregnant, she is humiliated. She wonders whether her parents ever have to know about her pregnancy. Her boyfriend tells her he will help her "take care of it."

_____

_____

5. "It will be fun," encouraged Jane. "We turn out the lights, sit on the floor in a circle, and invite ghosts and demons to make their presence known to us. We just do it for something to do. Can you come?"

_____

_____

He's by Our Side

Sixteen-year old Jack had received his license only two weeks earlier. On the way to the store, his father's car hit a slick spot on the pave-

But deliver us from evil.

But deliver us from evil.

What does this mean? We pray in this petition, in summary, that our Father in heaven would rescue us from every evil of body and soul, possessions and reputation, and finally, when our last hour comes, give us a blessed end, and graciously take us from this valley of sorrow to Himself in heaven.

The Growing Family

- Ask your parents to list specific examples of the protection and care God has provided to your family and/or to your grandparents or great-grandparents in days gone by.

- Talk with your parents about the temptations you face. Ask them to share with you about the temptations they contended with when they were your age and those temptations they face now. Pray together asking God to strengthen your family to resist temptations and to remain faithful to God.

With My Mentor

- Today with your mentor review the daily newspaper. Talk about the forces of evil evidenced in the world around you. Pray together asking God to protect you from all that would harm you or cause you to abandon your faith in Jesus.

- Talk with your mentor about the meaning of 2 Corinthians 12:9, "My grace is sufficient for you, for My power is made perfect in weakness." Invite your mentor to share with you what these words mean to him or her.

ment. Minutes later cars were parked at the side of the road and Jack and his dad, together with the drivers of the other cars, were talking to a policeman. The officer asked questions and made sure everyone had the proper insurance information they needed. Jack was at fault, yet he wasn't nervous or worried. His dad had been with him in the car when the accident happened. "Thanks for being here, Dad!" said Jack after the ordeal was over. Jack's father simply nodded and smiled.

Although bad things sometimes happen to the people of God, we need never doubt that, like Jack's father, Jesus is beside us to give us hope, comfort, and spiritual encouragement. Whatever we may face in life, He promises that nothing will ever separate us from His love and care for us.

1. What positive spiritual result does God desire to bring to us through the bad things that happen to us in our lives?

_____

_____

2. Into what kinds of evil do our spiritual enemies try to mislead us?

_____

_____

3. How does our Lord rescue us from every evil of body and soul, possessions, and reputation?

_____

_____

Writing Reflections

On the following lines, write a journal entry identifying some of the forces of evil that you recognize in the world around you. Then talk about the strong power of God and what Jesus means to you as you resist these forces by the strength the Holy Spirit gives you as you read and study God's Word.

_____

_____

_____

_____

_____

_____

_____

_____

_____

_____

Signed:_____ Date:_____

Responding to Our Awesome God

The Lord's Prayer
The Conclusion
Corporate Prayer

Praying Together

Confess your sins to each other and pray for each other so that you may be healed. The prayer of a righteous man is powerful and effective. James 5:16

Where Do You Go?

Think of the people in the picture below. All of them need some type of advice or assistance. Where would you encourage them to go for help? Why did you choose this place?

1. Celeste needs to set up a savings account.

_____

2. Carlos doesn't know what school district he lives in.

_____

3. Gayle wants to know the name of her state senator.

_____

4. Robin wants to buy a drum set.

_____

5. A Medieval monarch asks questions about God's kingdom.

_____

What evidence do you have that the places you have chosen for help would be able to help? Where do you go when you need help for problems too great for you to handle? Where do you go when you need forgiveness of sins? Where do you go when doctors say there is no hope?

Look at the following Bible verses. What do they tell you about God's ability to give you the help you need?

1. Ephesians 3:20

_____

_____

_____

2. Psalm 102:2–3

_____

_____

_____

3. Psalm 33:6

_____

_____

_____

The Conclusion

For Thine is the kingdom and the power and the glory forever and ever. Amen.

For the kingdom, the power, and the glory are Yours now and forever. Amen.

What does this mean? This means that I should be certain that these petitions are pleasing to our Father in heaven, and are heard by Him; for He Himself has commanded us to pray in this way and has promised to hear us. Amen, amen, which means "yes, yes, it shall be so."

Think about It

The closing to the Lord's Prayer reminds us that our God has power. He reigns and rules over heaven and earth. He reigns and rules over the kingdom that dwells in the hearts of all those who believe in Him. Those who believe in Him bow to His kingly power. They recognize that He hears and answers their prayers. They know that His answers are best for them, and they respond to His awesome answers to their prayers with worship and praise to such a wonderful God.

Read each of the following Bible sections with a partner. Pretend that you are a detective/reporter team. Your job is to discover the power and glory of God in each of the sections. Then you must seek out evidence of the response that greatness evokes from someone who has witnessed such power. Write about the event as if you were a news reporter covering the scene.

1. Mark 4:35–41

_____

2. Luke 18:35–42

_____

3. 1 Kings 18:20–39

_____

Discovery

Selma and Nao had planned the shopping trip for weeks. They would ride the train into New York and visit several of the large department stores. Then they would try to get some inexpensive tickets to the theater at one of the cut-rate ticket outlets. Of course, they knew they were taking a chance on that. The tickets might be sold out, and they might spend a quiet evening with no entertainment.

The train ride was uneventful. The landscape passed by at an amazing speed. It was interesting to see the countryside turn into city-scape. At last they were at their destination. The crowds were heavy but soon they hailed a taxi and were dropped off for their first shopping venture. The store was beautiful, and Selma found just the outfit she was looking for. Nao had more difficulty and decided she would just have to wait and look in the next store.

Out on the street people rushed by. Suddenly Nao felt a bump at her side. She quickly looked down and screamed with surprise. How could it be? Her purse was open and her wallet was gone. Nao's shoulders slumped. She felt hot tears come to her eyes. That was the end of her shopping adventure. Selma put her arms around Nao comfortingly. "It's okay, Nao," she said, "I have enough money for lunch and then we'll just head home."

"What's wrong, girls?" a kindly voice asked. The girls turned to see a kindly looking gentleman. "Step over here by this officer and let's hear the whole story."

Nao and Selma poured out their tale to the officer and the gentleman. They both nodded, knowingly. "I'm afraid your story is all too familiar. If you fill out a form, we'll keep our eyes out for your wallet, but the chances of its return are quite small," said the officer.

The gentleman spoke, "Girls, don't let this ruin your day in the city. Go into that store and pick out your outfit. Give them this card at the desk and, by the way, come and see the newest Broadway show as a treat from me."

As quick as the gentleman appeared he disappeared. The girls stood holding the card and glancing up at the officer. "Well, girls, someone is really looking out for you," said the officer. The girls glanced down at

- Get out old family photos or the family photo album. Take time to reminisce. What examples of answers to prayer and the greatness of God do you see in the life of your family? Pray together about things that are important to your family at this particular time.

- This lesson finishes the study of the Lord's Prayer. Use the Lord's Prayer today as the basis for your family devotion. After each petition give family members time to share, in their own words, just what that petition means to them. Then read the "What does this mean?" for each petition from the catechism.

- Ask your mentor to share examples of God's greatness and answered prayers from his or her own life. When has he or she seen that God's answers to their prayers were exactly what was best for him or her?

- Make a visit with your mentor to a shut-in or hospital. Talk together on the way about a prayer appropriate for the situation. Share this prayer as part of your visit.

the card. The message to the store and the theater were both signed by Broadway's biggest male lead.

The girls were overwhelmed by their bad experience turned good. They finished their shopping as told and ended up at the show with front and center seats.

When the girls got home …

How would you finish this story?

My Own Thoughts

1. How were the girls still able to have a great New York experience?

_____

_____

2. What might the girls have done in response to the star's kindness?

_____

_____

3. What things do we understand about our God when we approach His throne in prayer?

_____

_____

4. How do we respond to the gracious answers our God gives us when we pray?

_____

_____

Respond

Make a list of prayer requests that you have made to your great and powerful God. Why did you pray to Him? How did God answer your prayer? Pick one prayer request and answer that were particularly important to you. Write a letter to God praising Him for His greatness and power in answering all prayers.

_____

_____

_____

_____

_____

_____

_____

Signed:_____ Date:_____

Just the Beginning

The Sacrament of Holy Baptism

Welcome to God's Family

In their missionary journey to Europe, Paul and Silas were arrested. Acts 16:22–31 describes how God worked in their arrest and in the events that followed to bring one man and his entire family to faith.

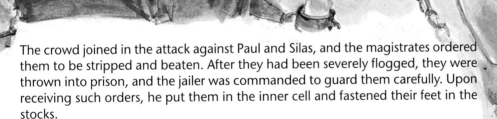

The crowd joined in the attack against Paul and Silas, and the magistrates ordered them to be stripped and beaten. After they had been severely flogged, they were thrown into prison, and the jailer was commanded to guard them carefully. Upon receiving such orders, he put them in the inner cell and fastened their feet in the stocks.

About midnight Paul and Silas were praying and singing hymns to God, and the other prisoners were listening to them. Suddenly there was such a violent earthquake that the foundations of the prison were shaken. At once all the prison doors flew open, and everybody's chains came loose. The jailer woke up, and when he saw the prison doors open, he drew his sword and was about to kill himself because he thought the prisoners had escaped. But Paul shouted, "Don't harm yourself! We are all here!"

The jailer called for lights, rushed in and fell trembling before Paul and Silas. He then brought them out and asked, "Sirs, what must I do to be saved?"

They replied, "Believe in the Lord Jesus, and you will be saved—you and your household." Acts 16:21–31

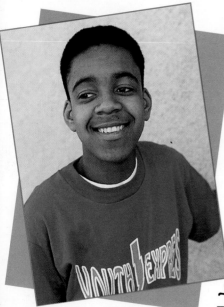

Baptism is more than water, banners, special songs and lots of pictures. It is a miracle that God performs to make people part of His family. By faith Baptism gives people life with God. The new life Jesus has won for us is indeed cause to celebrate.

Nothing Special?

"I'm nothing special," Joe always volunteers when asked to describe himself. "Just an 'Average Joe.'" Yet Joe is far from ordinary. Because of his faith in Jesus, he isn't afraid to stand alone if those around him are behaving in ways that he believes to be unhealthy for his relationship with Jesus. "When I am tempted to sin I remind myself that I am baptized," says Joe. Joe is a child of God.

1. What does it mean to be baptized?

for your sins to be washed away.

2. Who first instructed us to baptize people?

Jesus !

3. Who can baptize someone?

anybody who is chrischian !

4. Who should be baptized?

all people

5. What is given to a person in Baptism?

forjiviness of sins

6. Why was the Philippian jailer so happy?

because they didn't escape

7. When might it be especially helpful for you to remember "I am baptized"?

When I remember that I am a christian.

The Sacrament of Holy Baptism

What is Baptism?

Baptism is not just plain water, but it is water included in God's command and combined with God's Word.

Which is that word of God?

Christ our Lord says in the last chapter of Matthew: "Therefore go and make disciples of all nations, baptizing them in the name of the Father and of the Son and of the Holy Spirit." [Matt. 28:19]

What benefits does Baptism give?

It works forgiveness of sins, rescues from death and the devil, and gives eternal salvation to all who believe this, as the word and promises of God declare.

Which are these words and promises of God?

Christ our Lord says in the last chapter of Mark: "Whoever believes and is baptized will be saved, but whoever does not believe will be condemned." [Mark 16:16]

90

Verse Matt 28:19 Jesus told us to baptize

For Me!

Memories from the Baptism of *Ciara Annette McManus*

Date _____

Time _____

Location _____

Pastor _____

Weather _____

Sponsors _____

What the family did after the baptismal service.

_____

Who was there.

_____

Other special memories.

_____
_____
_____
_____
_____

Place photo taken on the day of your Baptism here.

The Growing Family

- As a family complete the section, "Baptismal Memories." If you have not been baptized, use the sheet as a planning guide for what you would like the day to include.

- Create a collection of pictures from the day you were baptized. The pictures may also include other baptisms in the family. Bring these to class to share as part of the opening.

With My Mentor

- Ask your mentor to share about the importance Baptism plays in his or her personal life. Share what Baptism means to you.

- Together with your mentor, write a letter to a family who has recently had someone baptized in the church. Share with your mentor any personal thoughts about Baptism and its blessings.

Signed: _____ Date: _____

25

H₂O + GOD = AWESOME!

The Sacrament of Holy Baptism

Baptism Power

At one time we too were foolish, disobedient, deceived and enslaved by all kinds of passions and pleasures. We lived in malice and envy, being hated and hating one another. But when the kindness and love of God our Savior appeared, He saved us, not because of righteous things we had done, but because of His mercy. He saved us through the washing of rebirth and renewal by the Holy Spirit, whom He poured out on us generously through Jesus Christ our Savior, so that, having been justified by His grace, we might become heirs having the hope of eternal life. This is a trustworthy saying. And I want you to stress these things, so that those who have trusted in God may be careful to devote themselves to doing what is good. These things are excellent and profitable for everyone. Titus 3:3–8

God's Word is what gives Baptism its power. This power is part of our daily lives.

Long ago, by inspiration of the Holy Spirit, St. Paul wrote to Titus about the ways God's grace and power can be shown in the life of the Christian. As a pastor, Titus reminded the congregation to be subject to rulers and authorities, to be obedient, to be ready to do whatever is good, to slander no one, to be peaceable and considerate, and to show true humility toward all people.

As you reflect on this portion from Titus 3, write *Old* before each of the behaviors that show the influence of the Old Person. Write *New* before each of the behaviors that describe the New Person God makes us by the power of the Holy Spirit.

_____ 1. Disobedience

_____ 2. Thinking good thoughts about situations and other people

_____ 3. Gossip

_____ 4. Kindness

_____ 5. Helpfulness

_____ 6. Cheerfulness

_____ 7. Patience

_____ 8. Slander

_____ 9. Hatred

_____ 10. Generosity

What Baptism Does for Our Daily Life

Answer the following questions about the *Old Adam* and the *New Man*.

1. What is the Old Adam?

_____

_____

2. How is this Old Adam to be drowned in us?

_____

_____

3. What is the new man?

_____

_____

4. How is this new man to emerge and arise?

_____

_____

Issues Now

In a quiet corner of a cemetery in the eastern part of the United States, a tombstone bears the following simple message:
> Jeffrey Winterton
> 1976–1996
> "If anyone is in Christ,
>   he is a new creation."

Speculate on Jeffrey's life story and what these words may have meant to him in his life. Then comment on what they mean to him now.

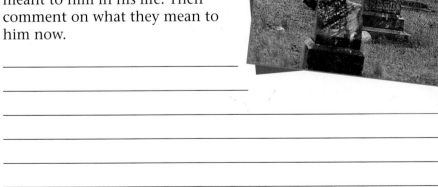

_____

_____

_____

_____

_____

_____

The Sacrament of Holy Baptism

How can water do such great things?

Certainly not just water, but the word of God in and with the water does these things, along with the faith which trusts this word of God in the water. For without God's word the water is plain water and no Baptism. But with the word of God it is a Baptism, that is, a life-giving water, rich in grace, and a washing of the new birth in the Holy Spirit, as St. Paul says in Titus chapter three: "He saved us through the washing of rebirth and renewal by the Holy Spirit, whom He poured out on us generously through Jesus Christ our Savior, so that, having been justified by His grace, we might become heirs having the hope of eternal life. This is a trustworthy saying." [Titus 3:5–8]

What does such baptizing with water indicate?

It indicates that the Old Adam should by daily contrition and repentance be drowned and die with all sins and evil desires, and that a new man should daily emerge and arise to live before God in righteousness and purity forever.

Where is this written?

St. Paul writes in Romans chapter six: "We were therefore buried with Him through baptism into death in order that, just as Christ was raised from the dead through the glory of the Father, we too may live a new life." [Rom. 6:4]

The Growing Family

- As a family discuss how Christians can live the faith into which they were baptized so that others see their lights shining.

- Look for a service project you can do as a family either at church or in your community. As you and your family complete it together, praise God for the new people He has made you through Jesus, the Savior, into whose family you have been baptized.

With My Mentor

- Share with your mentor what you have written in the "Living the New Life" section of this lesson. Allow your mentor to encourage you to live out your commitment to daily living for the Lord.

- Join with your mentor in the challenge in identifying specific ways to live out the new life you received from your Baptism and the Word of God.

Living the New Life

Write a paragraph to complete each of the two statements below. You will be asked to share what you have written with another student in your class and with your mentor. The lines at the bottom of the page are for your signature, your partner's signature, and/or your mentor's signature.

"Because of the power of God given in my Baptism, I am able to ..."

_____
_____
_____
_____
_____
_____
_____
_____

"Because of the power of God given to me in my Baptism, I am committed to ..."

_____
_____
_____
_____
_____
_____
_____

I pray for the power to daily live and grow before God in true faith and good works.

Signed:_____ Signed:_____

I will pray that _____ has the power to daily live and grow before God in true faith and good works.

_____
_____

Signed:_____ Date:_____

94

26

The Gift of Forgiveness

Confession and Absolution
The Office of the Keys

An Awesome Gift

King David was a great leader of God's people. He was also a sinful human being. 2 Samuel 11 contains a story that might rival any seen on a television soap opera. The difference is that in David's case what happened was very real.

The good news is that David experienced God's forgiveness in a very real and dramatic way. The experience reminded David how he, on a daily basis, was being touched by God's forgiving hand.

Check out the following Scripture references to discover what sins David committed and how God responded to David's actions.

2 Samuel 11:2–5 Sin no. 1 _____

2 Samuel 11:14–16 Sin no. 2 _____

2 Samuel 12:1–9 Nathan Confronts David

2 Samuel 12:13a David's Response _____

2 Samuel 12:13b God's Response _____

Confession

What is confession?

Confession has two parts.

First that we confess our sins, and

second, that we receive absolution, that is, forgiveness, from the pastor as from God Himself, not doubting, but firmly believing that by it our sins are forgiven before God in heaven.

What sins should we confess?

Before God we should plead guilty of all sins, even those we are not aware of, as we do in the Lord's Prayer; but before the pastor we should confess only those sins which we know and feel in our hearts.

Which are these?

Consider your place in life according to the Ten Commandments: Are you a father, mother, son, daughter, husband, wife, or worker? Have you been disobedient, unfaithful, or lazy? Have you been hot-tempered, rude, or quarrelsome? Have you hurt someone by your words or deeds? Have you stolen, been negligent, wasted anything, or done any harm?

Responding to the Good News

God's Good News to King David gave the king a reason for celebration. David's thoughts are recorded in Psalm 51. God has the same message of forgiveness for each of us as His baptized children. Check out David's response to God and then, using David's example, write your own response to God.

David's Response	My Response

Psalm 51:1 Have mercy on me, O God,
according to Your
unfailing love; blot out
my transgressions

Psalm 51:2 Wash away all my iniquity
and cleanse me from my sin.

Psalm 51:3 For I know my
transgressions
and my sin is always
before me.

Psalm 51:4 Against You, You only, have I
sinned and done what is evil in
Your sight, so that You are
proved right when You speak
and justified when You judge.

Psalm 51:5 Surely I was sinful at birth,
sinful from the time my
mother conceived me.

Psalm 51:6 Surely You desire truth in
the inner parts;
You teach me wisdom in
the inmost place.

Psalm 51:7 Cleanse me with hyssop, and
I will be clean;
wash me, and I will be
whiter than snow.

Signed:_____ Date:_____

Keys of the Kingdom

What is the Office of the Keys?

The Office of the Keys is that special authority which Christ has given to His church on earth to forgive the sins of repentant sinners, but to withhold forgiveness from the unrepentant as long as they do not repent.

Where is this written?

This is what St. John the Evangelist writes in chapter twenty: The Lord Jesus breathed on His disciples and said, "Receive the Holy Spirit. If you forgive anyone his sins, they are forgiven; if you do not forgive them, they are not forgiven." [John 20:22–23]

What do you believe according to these words?

I believe that when the called ministers of Christ deal with us by His divine command, in particular when they exclude openly unrepentant sinners from the Christian congregation and absolve those who repent of their sins and want to do better, this is just as valid and certain, even in heaven, as if Christ our dear Lord dealt with us Himself.

Christ Delivering the Keys of the Kingdom to St. Peter

Forgiveness Comes Home

Titus really loved his dad. Since his parents had divorced, he seldom saw his father. The Little League season was half over and his dad had yet to see him play. Memories of evenings spent playing catch in the

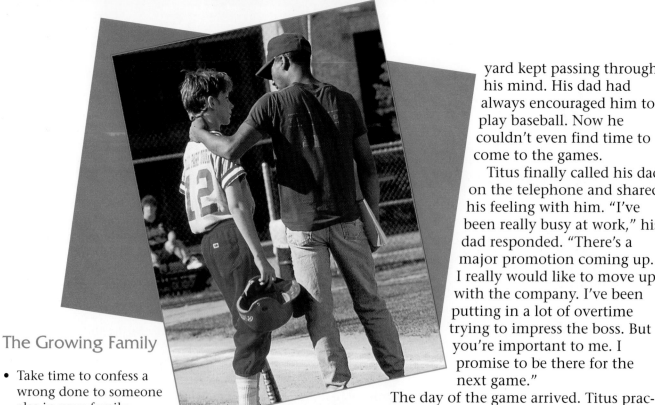

The Growing Family

- Take time to confess a wrong done to someone else in your family. Allow other family members to do the same. Then celebrate the forgiveness Jesus has earned for you and for each member of your family.

- Read aloud the story of Titus and his dad entitled "Forgiveness Comes Home." As a family discuss the questions at the conclusion of the story. Offer a prayer of thanksgiving for Christ's forgiveness in your lives.

With My Mentor

- Think about the relationship that has developed between you and your mentor. Talk with your mentor about ways that he or she has been helpful to you.

- Talk with your mentor about the power of Christ's forgiveness in his or her life.

yard kept passing through his mind. His dad had always encouraged him to play baseball. Now he couldn't even find time to come to the games.

Titus finally called his dad on the telephone and shared his feeling with him. "I've been really busy at work," his dad responded. "There's a major promotion coming up. I really would like to move up with the company. I've been putting in a lot of overtime trying to impress the boss. But you're important to me. I promise to be there for the next game."

The day of the game arrived. Titus practiced extra hard before the game. He wanted to be ready to do his best. The time for the game arrived, and he surveyed the stands but he didn't see one familiar face. "He'll be here. He promised," he thought to himself as he stepped to the plate the first time. Titus struck out, and when he returned to the bench he was angry. "A promise is a promise," he thought.

Titus had a terrible game. He not only didn't get a hit but made a crucial error in the field. His team lost by a wide margin, and he could tell the coach was disappointed.

Titus got on his bike and headed home. He was shocked when he reached his driveway to find a familiar car parked in front of the house. His dad got out and walked toward him. "I'm sorry I missed the game. I had to work late again but before I left I told my boss that it was the last time. I like my job, and while the promotion would be nice, watching you play baseball is more important. I don't want to miss another game this season. Will you forgive me?

Questions for Discussion:

1. What choice does Titus have? What reasons does he have to forgive his father? What reasons does he have to not forgive him?

2. How will Titus' decision affect his future relationship with his father?

3. What risk is involved if Titus *does* forgive his father?

4. How does Titus' forgiveness of his father illustrate God's forgiveness toward us?

5. Why do we need to take the risk by being willing to forgive others even when their sins have hurt us?

27

Showing Love to the Unrepentant

Church Discipline and Excommunication

Faithful and Just

If we claim to be without sin, we deceive ourselves and the truth is not in us. If we confess our sins, He is faithful and just and will forgive us our sins and purify us from all unrighteousness. 1 John 1:8–9

Trouble among Friends

José and Manuel looked at the graffiti spray-painted on the store front. It wasn't hard to believe that someone had vandalized Señor Aguilar's store again. What was hard to believe was that their friend Pedro admitted doing it.

The three boys became friends during the summer's vacation Bible school held at San Pablo Lutheran Mission. Pastor Segovia also became their special friend. The three boys found a common bond in their desire to not become part of the gangs that controlled their community. Pedro had seen his brother killed in a gang-related drive-by shooting. He said he wanted no part of that culture.

Pastor Segovia encouraged them to start their own club. They met with him regularly to discuss ways that they could help their community. Pastor Segovia also taught them more about Jesus. He instructed them in the catechism. Manuel began serving as an acolyte one Sunday a month. The other boys wanted to join him.

Señor Aguilar also became their friend. His store was a frequent target of vandalism. It started when he discontinued selling liquor and cigarettes. He also took a stand against the drug problem. He no longer allowed people to loiter around his store

front. The three boys helped him by cleaning up the outside of his store. They helped other merchants too but Señor Aguilar had become special to them.

They knew he appreciated their work. He often gave them free cans of soda pop from the cooler in exchange for their help.

The two boys did not hear Pastor Segovia come up behind them until he placed his arm on their shoulders. "What are you boys going to do?" he asked.

"I suppose we need to clean it off," replied Jesse. "It's just hard knowing that Pedro did it."

"Have you asked him why?" Pastor Segovia responded. "I know Pedro still carries a lot of anger over his brother's murder."

"He says that Señor Aguilar cheated him, yesterday," reported Manuel. "He bought a candy bar, and it was stale. Señor Aguilar would not give him his money back. I would have bought him another candy bar if he would have asked me. I can't believe he did this."

"I guess this is the end of our club," remarked José. "It's difficult to have a club with two people. Besides, even if he says he's sorry, there is no guarantee it won't happen again."

"I know you boys talked to him alone, and he wouldn't listen. Maybe it would help if I went with you," suggested the pastor. "That's what Jesus told His disciples to do in Matthew 18:15–17. If Pedro says he's sorry we have no choice except to forgive him. If he still isn't sorry, then we have a problem. But we have to try."

1. Did Manuel and José have a reason to be angry with Pedro? Why?

_____

_____

_____

_____

_____

2. Read Matthew 18:15–17. According to Jesus, if someone sins what three steps are to be followed?

Step 1:

_____

_____

Step 2:

_____

_____

Step 3:

_____

_____

The Growing Family

- As a family discuss the three situations in the Applying the Word section. Talk about how to apply the three steps outlined in Matthew 18. Reflect on similar situations that may have occurred in your family or among those you know. Emphasize the power of Christ's forgiveness in dealing with human failings and conflicts.

- Review the Activity Sheet with your parents. Talk together about how the authority and responsibility God has given us affect the relationships we share with family and friends.

3. Jesus told His followers to "treat an unrepentant sinner as they would a pagan or a tax collector." How did the early church treat such people? See Matthew 9:10–11 and Luke 5:29–30.

_____

_____

4. See Galatians 6:1–2. According to St. Paul, what responsibility does the church have toward a person caught in sin?

_____

_____

5. What should happen if Pedro continues to be unrepentant? Check 1 Corinthians 5:13.

_____

_____

6. What should happen if Pedro confesses his sin and asks to be a member of the club again? See St. Paul's instructions in 2 Corinthians 2:7–8.

_____

_____

The Church's Responsibility

God has given His church on earth an awesome responsibility. "I tell you the truth, whatever you bind on earth will be bound in heaven." Matthew 18:18

Pedro has admitted painting graffiti on Señor Aguilar's store. If he continues to refuse to repent of that sin, what obligation do José and Manuel, representing the church, have?

What obligation does Pastor Segovia have as a leader of God's people? See catechism questions 280–282. Use the space below to write what you feel his responsibility is.

_____

_____

What is the purpose of that action according to catechism question 283?

_____

_____

"Be completely humble and gentle; be patient, bearing with one another in love. Make every effort to keep the unity of the Spirit through the bond of peace." Ephesians 4:2–3.

With My Mentor

- With your mentor read Ephesians 4:2–3. Four characteristics of discipleship are listed in the first sentence: humility, gentleness, patience, and forbearance/mercy. God's desire is expressed in the second sentence, "… keep the unity of the Spirit through the bond of peace." Talk together about how these characteristics reveal God's purpose for His chosen people in Christ. Discuss models of peacemaking that they have seen in their lives.

- Together with your mentor review the entire Confession section of the catechism, stressing the power of God's love and forgiveness for our daily lives.

Applying the Word

Jesus' word in Matthew 18:15–17 has a powerful, far-reaching effect upon our daily lives. One area, in particular, is relationships within our family. What might happen in each of the following situations if Jesus' instructions are followed?

1. Tanya keeps borrowing her sister's CD's without permission. Their mother has threatened to ground her for a month. Her sister has discovered another CD missing. She wonders if she should go directly to her mother.

_____

_____

2. Sidney's dad keeps promising to take him to a baseball game but he always finds excuses. Sidney's feelings are really hurt. He wonders if he should talk to his mother about his feelings.

_____

_____

3. Carolyn found out that her older brother has gotten into trouble at school. The principal has threatened to suspend him if it happens again. On the way home from school she discusses with her friends whether she should tell their mother about the situation. Her good friend Carla has offered to go with her if she wants to talk to her brother first.

_____

_____

Dear Jaymie,

We are running this letter in the paper because it's been three weeks now since we've seen you last. We don't know whether you are safe. We don't even know where you are. We needed to talk with you about the way you were living because we love you and care about you. Now we are worried sick about you. We love you and want you back in our family. Won't you call home? You know the number. Mom and Dad, Jennie, Bruce, and Mark.

On the lines below write something personal you would want Jaymie to know if you were her brother or sister.

_____

_____

_____

_____

_____

Signed:_____ Date:_____

28

God's Wonderful Meal

The Sacrament of the Altar

Bread of Life

They devoted themselves to the apostles' teaching and to the fellowship, to the breaking of bread and to prayer. Acts 2:42

A Meal to Remember

Billy looked down at the letter he had just received from his brother Mark. He remembered the last time he had seen Mark—just three weeks ago. It was Mark's final night before leaving to join the service.

The Sacrament of the Altar

What is the Sacrament of the Altar?

It is the true body and blood of our Lord Jesus Christ under the bread and wine, instituted by Christ Himself for us Christians to eat and to drink.

Where is this written?

The holy Evangelists Matthew, Mark, Luke, and St. Paul write:

Our Lord Jesus Christ, on the night when He was betrayed, took bread, and when He had given thanks, He broke it and gave it to the disciples and said: "Take, eat; this is My body, which is given for you. This do in remembrance of Me."

In the same way also He took the cup after supper, and when He had given thanks, He gave it to them, saying, "Drink of it, all of you; this cup is the new testament in My blood, which is shed for you for the forgiveness of sins. This do, as often as you drink it, in remembrance of Me."

What is the benefit of this eating and drinking?

These words, "Given and shed for you for the forgiveness of sins," show us that in the Sacrament forgiveness of sins, life, and salvation are given us through these words. For where there is forgiveness of sins, there is also life and salvation.

Their Mom had prepared his favorite meal—steak, with macaroni and cheese, and apple pie. She had invited their grandparents, aunts, uncles, and all their cousins, and a good number of Mark's closest friends from school. The gathering was large, yet an intimate affair; Mark, of course, was the guest of honor. Everyone knew that Mark was ready to begin the greatest adventure of his life. Even as he ate that night in the company of his family and friends, Mark's thoughts were on the day ahead and the journey that would take him far away from home.

1. Why was the family's meal together so memorable?
2. What were the "benefits" of eating the meal together?
3. What are the benefits of the Lord's Supper?

Discover the Benefits

A. Forgiveness of Sins

B. Life and salvation

C. Victory over sin

D. Public confession/unity

Jesus' Last Will and Testament

I, Christ Jesus, being of sound mind and body, do hereby make my last will and testament. I freely give the following …

To _____ I give you My body. Do this in remembrance of me.

(your name)_____

To _____ I give you My blood. Do this in remembrance of me.

(your name)_____

Where to Find These Precious Words

Read the following verses and note the information each provides about Jesus' last will and testament.

1. Matthew 26:17–30

_____

_____

_____

_____

2. Mark 14:12–26, Luke 22:7–38

_____

_____

_____

_____

3. 1 Corinthians 11:23–26

_____

_____

_____

_____

Forgiveness through the Sacrament

On the lines below tell what the forgiveness offered in the Lord's Supper means to you.

_____

_____

_____

_____

_____

_____

_____

_____

_____

_____

Signed:_____ Date:_____

The Growing Family

• Talk about special meals and events you have enjoyed together as a family. Talk about a significant memory you have about a celebration of the Lord's Supper. Thank God together for the blessing He offers through this special meal.

• Use a recipe to make unleavened bread together as a family project. While the bread is baking, read through the following verses to discover why we use unleavened bread for Holy Communion: Exodus 12:1–39 and Mark 14:12–26.

With My Mentor

• Talk with your mentor about the Lord's Supper. Ask him or her, What was your most memorable celebration of the Lord's Supper? Why was it so special to you? When do you most desire Holy Communion? What does it mean to you to participate in the body and blood of Christ (1 Corinthians 10:16–17)?

• Interview members in your congregation about communion and its value for their Christian life. Then talk with your mentor about the results of your interview.

29
The Lord's Supper
The Sacrament of the Altar

Paul Writes

For I received from the Lord what I also passed on to you: The Lord Jesus, on the night He was betrayed, took bread, and when He had given thanks, He broke it and said, "This is My body, which is for you; do this in remembrance of Me." In the same way, after supper He took the cup, saying, "This cup is the new covenant in My blood; do this, whenever you drink it, in remembrance of Me." For whenever you eat this bread and drink this cup, you proclaim the Lord's death until He comes.

Therefore, whoever eats the bread or drinks the cup of the Lord in an unworthy manner will be guilty of sinning against the body and blood of the Lord. A man ought to examine himself before he eats of the bread and drinks of the cup. For anyone who eats and drinks without recognizing the body of the Lord eats and drinks judgment on himself. 1 Corinthians 11:23–29

1. Underline Jesus' words of institution in the verses above.
2. Circle the words from the verses indicating that the Sacrament of the Altar is to be taken seriously by those who partake of it.
3. Draw a cross beside the words that indicate what Christians are doing when they attend the Lord's Supper.

Great-Grandma Remembers

Rachel was restless. First she walked back and forth across the family room. Then she sat down on the recliner. Finally she sprawled out on the floor. Clearly she was restless. This assignment was tough! "Great-Grandma?" she asked, as she stood and approached the elderly woman sitting on the sofa. "What does it mean to prepare to receive the Lord's Supper?"

Her great-grandmother looked up from her book. "To prepare to receive the Sacrament means to ask yourself whether you trust in Jesus as your Savior. It means to think about your sins and your desire to live for Christ." Her quick and direct responses always intrigued Rachel. She was sharp as a tack, she thought to herself. She listened for more, knowing more would follow. With Great-grandma, it always did.

"I remember, though," she went on, "that my parents always went to the home of the pastor during the week before taking communion. They went to confess their sins privately to God and to receive the assurance of the forgiveness of sins from the pastor. Then on Sunday they had special clothes they wore only on Communion Sundays. They didn't eat breakfast on Sunday before going to communion, either."

Receiving the Benefits

What do Christians believe about the Sacrament of the Altar? How do we receive forgiveness of sins through Holy Communion? (See "The Power of the Sacrament of the Altar," Catechism, p. 236)

I believe

_____

_____

I receive

_____

_____

Preparing to Receive the Sacrament

Important Information Regarding the Following: These questions and answers are no child's play, but are drawn up with great earnestness of purpose by the venerable and devout Dr. Luther for both young and old. Let each one pay

The Sacrament of the Altar

How can bodily eating and drinking do such great things?

Certainly not just eating and drinking do these things, but the words written here: "Given and shed for you for the forgiveness of sins." These words, along with the bodily eating and drinking, are the main thing in the Sacrament. Whoever believes these words has exactly what they say: "forgiveness of sins."

Who receives this sacrament worthily?

Fasting and bodily preparation are certainly fine outward training. But that person is truly worthy and well prepared who has faith in these words: "Given and shed for you for the forgiveness of sins."

But anyone who does not believe these words or doubts them is unworthy and unprepared, for the words "for you" require all hearts to believe.

attention and consider it a serious matter; for St. Paul writes to the Galatians in chapter six: "Do not be deceived: God cannot be mocked."

Luther's words invite us to reflect thoughtfully upon the Lord's gifts in the Sacrament of the Altar. Answer the following questions sincerely, applying each personally.

1. Do you believe that you are a sinner?

_____

2. How do you know this?

_____

3. Are you sorry for your sins?

_____

4. What have you deserved from God because of your sins?

_____

_____

5. Do you hope to be saved?

_____

6. In whom then do you trust?

_____

7. Who is Christ?

_____

_____

8. How many Gods are there?

_____

9. What has Christ done for you that you trust in Him?

_____

_____

10. Did the Father also die for you?

_____

_____

11. How do you know this?

_____

_____

The Growing Family

• Think about and adopt "traditions" for Holy Communion. As a family, sit together on Communion Sundays and receive the Sacrament as a family. As you return to your seats, hold hands to demonstrate your unity. Write a family prayer that thanks God for the Lord's Supper; say it before you travel to church. Create a prayer for after Holy Communion, including thanksgiving, praise, and a request for God's strength to live as faithful servants. Have family members pray that prayer silently after communion.

• Create a collage that represents unity and traditions you have as a family, using magazine pictures, photographs, objects, or drawings. Include taking communion or going to church together as a family to be a part of the collage.

12. What are the words of institution?

_____

_____

13. Do you believe, then, that the true body and blood of Christ are in the Sacrament?

_____

_____

14. What convinces you to believe this?

_____

_____

15. What should we do when we eat His body and drink His blood, and in this way receive His pledge?

_____

_____

16. Why should we remember and proclaim His death?

_____

_____

17. What motivated Christ to die and make full payment for your sins?

_____

_____

18. Finally, why do you wish to go to the Sacrament?

_____

_____

19. What should admonish and encourage a Christian to receive the Sacrament frequently?

_____

_____

20. But what should you do if you are not aware of this need and have no hunger and thirst for the Sacrament?

_____

_____

_____

Signed:_____ Date:_____

With My Mentor

- Together with your mentor, visit shut-ins in your congregation. If the shut-ins you visit enjoy talking about their faith, ask, "How long have you been a Christian?" "Do you remember your confirmation?" "What does taking communion mean to you?" "What is your favorite memory of the church?" Usually shut-ins enjoy having a young person around and love to tell stories about their life.

- Contact your mentor or an elder of the congregation to ask "What things should you do to prepare for Holy Communion?" Review with him or her what you have written in this section of the Response Book.

30

My Christian Faith

Conclusion

The Missing Part

The body is a unit, though it is made up of many parts; and though all its parts are many, they form one body. So it is with Christ. ... Now the body is not made up of one part but of many. If the foot should say, "Because I am not a hand, I do not belong to the body," it would not for that reason cease to be a part of the body. And if the ear should say, "Because I am not an eye, I do not belong to the body," it would not for that reason cease to be a part of the body. ... Now you are the body of Christ, and each one of you is a part of it." 1 Corinthians 12:12, 14–16, 27

Kristine's family comes to your church about one Sunday each month. She attends a school in the next school district and doesn't really know anyone from your class, even though she is in the same grade. Sometimes she attends your Sunday school class, but just sits quietly and doesn't say very much. She is usually friendly, but shy, and talks mostly about her friends from school.

A few months ago she came to a junior high fun night at your church, but she isn't very athletic and didn't seem to enjoy the games. She didn't sing during the worship because, she said, "I don't have a good voice." The members of your group were nice to her, but it was difficult because you don't know her that well.

Recently you saw her at the mall, said "hello," and had a friendly visit with her. She asked how the kids at church were doing and you said, "They're great! I wish you would join us more often!"

Kristine said, "I just don't fit in with the church."

You didn't know what to say, so you talked a little longer and then said good-bye. Since you got home, you've been thinking about her and have decided to write a note to encourage her to be a part of the group.

Write the note to Kristine.

_____

_____

_____

_____

_____

Looking for Evidence

One of your classmates from school claims to be the number 1 fan of your hometown team, the Turtleville Snappers. You have been appointed by the local booster club to watch him and carefully determine if there is any evidence to prove that he is indeed the number 1 fan.

If you were to follow him for a week and examine his personal belongings, what kinds of evidence would you expect to gather if he were indeed the number 1 fan? Make a list of what you might find.

_____

_____

_____

_____

What evidence would you expect to find in the life of a Christian that would prove that their faith was an important part of their life? Try to think of at least four or five examples before you turn to the Bible for help.

John 13:35

_____

_____

James 2:14–17

_____

_____

Hebrews 10:25

_____

_____

Acts 2:42–47

_____

_____

John 13:12–17

_____

_____

Ephesians 2:10

_____

_____

The Growing Family

- Share with your family the plan that you have designed for your spiritual growth as a member of the body of Christ.

- Using the same categories as in your own personal plan for growth, lead your family in setting some goals—this time as applied to family life. Discuss ways that your family can grow together through worship, Bible study, and servanthood. Realize that your family is connected to something bigger than itself—the whole family of believers—the body of Christ. Consider ways that you, together as a family, could serve others, such as serving at a food bank or becoming involved in the life and work of a missionary.

- Suggest a family meeting centered around the topic of church membership. What are the parents' histories of church membership? How about the grandparents? In what way have the churches to which they belonged been communities of faith and support?

Matthew 25:34–36

_____

_____

My Plan for Growing In Faith

Now that you are near the end of this Response Book and this course, you should think about your continuing growth in your Christian faith. As you learned in this course, God the Holy Spirit works in the lives of God's people to create and strengthen faith through the Lord's body and blood, received in Holy Communion, personal Bible study and Bible study with other Christians. Worship with other Christians is vital for a growing faith.

Another part of keeping your faith alive and growing is service to others. Use the space below to make a commitment along with the other members of your group for the next three weeks. Consider how important it is to do something similar on a regular basis throughout your life as a Christian.

When you have completed setting your goals in each category, sign and date your covenant form and have a witness from your class sign it with you.

My worship life:

My daily Bible reading:

My Bible study with other Christians:

My daily prayer time:

Service to my family:

Service to my church:

Service to my community:

Signed _____ Date _____

Witness _____

Jesus said, "Everyone who hears these words of mine and puts them into practice is like a wise man who built his house on the rock."
Matthew 7:24

With My Mentor

- Ask your mentor what it means to him or her to be a "responsible church member."

- Discuss with your mentor, What makes his or her devotional life important and meaningful. Are there times when keeping a consistent devotional life is a struggle? What benefits does he or she receive from regularly turning to the Lord in devotion and prayer?

112